RECLAIMING YOUR
IDENTITY

EMBRACE WHO GOD CREATED YOU TO BE

ERIC WAYMAN

WESTBOW
PRESS®
A DIVISION OF THOMAS NELSON
& ZONDERVAN

This book is a work of non-fiction. Unless otherwise noted, the author and the publisher make no explicit guarantees as to the accuracy of the information contained in this book and in some cases, names of people and places have been altered to protect their privacy.

WestBow Press books may be ordered through booksellers or by contacting:

WestBow Press
A Division of Thomas Nelson & Zondervan
1663 Liberty Drive
Bloomington, IN 47403
www.westbowpress.com
1 (866) 928-1240

Because of the dynamic nature of the Internet, any web addresses or links contained in this book may have changed since publication and may no longer be valid. The views expressed in this work are solely those of the author and do not necessarily reflect the views of the publisher, and the publisher hereby disclaims any responsibility for them.

Any people depicted in stock imagery provided by Thinkstock are models, and such images are being used for illustrative purposes only. Certain stock imagery © Thinkstock.

ISBN: 978-1-9736-0757-1 (sc)
ISBN: 978-1-9736-0758-8 (hc)
ISBN: 978-1-9736-0756-4 (e)

Library of Congress Control Number: 2017919255

Print information available on the last page.

WestBow Press rev. date: 02/1/2018

For my sons, Ethan and Grayson -
It brings me so much joy to help you grow into
the men that God has created you to be.
I am proud to be your father.

CONTENTS

PART 1
Warped Images

CHAPTER 1

Who Do You Think You Are?

What is your name?
-Jesus

As the bow of the small fishing boat scraped up onto the rocky shore, a dozen exhausted men piled out, grateful to have firm ground under their feet once again. The last night had been a rough one, even for the fishermen among them who had grown up on these waters. In the middle of the night, as they had sailed their little boat across the Sea of Galilee, a furious storm had picked up. At one point the men aboard had concluded that they would never reach shore, and that their little vessel would be swamped by the wind-swept waves.

Yet here they were, back on solid ground. All because their teacher had intervened, waking up at the last moment and commanding the storm to quiet down. Despite all they'd seen, and despite all Jesus had done in the short time they had been following him, this was undoubtedly the most amazing miracle yet. Even the wind and waves obeyed him.

The disciples stretched their weary legs and began to make their way up the beach and into the unfamiliar territory of the Gerasenes. They had landed on a small beach, nestled between a rocky shoal on one side and a gentle hill ending in a cliff on the other. A herd of pigs dotted the hillside, foraging for food in the rain-soaked soil. Up ahead of them, they spied a number of caves cut into the hillside - evidence that they'd landed near a cemetery.

Rabbi Jesus led them toward the nearest town, looking surprisingly rested in light of what they'd just been through. Then again, he was the only one who had gotten any sleep last night. As they passed the caves, a primal scream shattered the stillness of the morning and stopped them in their tracks.

The small group glanced around nervously, searching for the source of the cry. A disheveled man emerged from one of the tombs cut into the hillside and shambled toward them, yelling incoherently as he came. A couple of the disciples moved in front of their rabbi, taking up a defensive posture. Then as the madman drew near, Jesus spoke with the same calm authority that he'd used to quiet the storm. "Come out of this man, you evil spirit."

The raving man stopped short as if he'd been struck in the face. He fell to his knees less than a dozen paces from the bewildered group. His clothing was nothing more than filthy rags, his arms were covered in jagged, weeping wounds that attracted the flies, and he smelled like an open grave. Even from this distance the foul odor was overpowering, and several of the disciples reflexively covered their noses.

Suddenly the madman looked right at Jesus and screamed, "I know who you are, Son of God!" His feral eyes betrayed a hint of fear mixed with madness as he spoke. "Swear to the Creator that you won't torture me!"

Jesus looked compassionately at the man groveling in the dust before him, and in an unexpectedly gentle voice he asked him, "What is your name?"

****

What Is Your Name?

What a surprising question given the circumstances. Jesus is in a completely foreign territory, confronted by a raving lunatic on the outskirts of a cemetery, and he wants to know this guy's name?

Even more surprising is how the man responds. He could have answered with the name his parents had given him. Or with a nickname. But he didn't use any of those. Instead he chooses to identify himself by his greatest source of torment.

"My name is Legion," he replied to Jesus's query, "because of the number of demons inside of me."

This man, who had been tormented by his demons and rejected by his own people, identified himself by his brokenness. In his eyes, he *was* his brokenness. And despite the fact that his story appears in three of the four gospels, we never actually learn his name; he is known only as "the demon-possessed man" or "the Gerasene Demoniac."

Can you identify with him? I don't mean the demon-possession part, but are you tempted to define yourself by your brokenness? I sure am. Looking back over my life, it seems that far too often my victory celebrations have been short-lived, but my failures just kept coming back to haunt my thoughts. They stick in the back of my mind like a sliver under the skin, demanding that I rehash them over and over again. Similarly, the affirmations that people have given me tend to roll over me like a sweet fragrance on the breeze, here one moment and gone the next, but their critiques cut to my heart like a rifle bullet. Do you know what I mean?

Far too many of us carry around our mistakes and the hurtful things people have said to us as if they were rocks in a backpack. Though they don't necessarily debilitate us, they sure do weigh us down. They can even begin to hinder us from living the life of freedom that our Creator intended for us. As a pastor, I can't even begin to count the number of conversations I've had with people wrestling with an overwhelming sense of inadequacy. They look at their shortcomings and conclude that they are defined by them—that they are a failure, a disappointment, a reject. I understand the feeling. I've spent far too much of my life haunted by the same thoughts.

Proving Your Worth

Perhaps you go the other way. You don't let your mistakes and failures define you; instead, you let your victories and successes do the talking. Maybe you've come to believe that you are the sum total of what you've accomplished and accumulated. You proclaim your identity through the clothes you wear, the car you drive, and the title on your business cards. You find your value in the respect you garner from those around you, even if you know deep down that you're not as put together as people think you are. But what they don't know doesn't define you, right? So you bury your faults under layers of activity and you prove your worth through what you do.

Admittedly, even this approach to life can be exhausting and debilitating.

A friend of mine was pigeonholed as the good kid in her family. Because of her sweet temperament and obedient nature, her mother would often tell her that she was a perfect child. Ironically, this affirmation became a burden that she had to carry around with her. Though it was intended to build her up, it only weighed her down with an unrealistic expectation that she felt obligated to meet. So when she tried something that she didn't naturally excel at, like a new sport, she would quickly give up because it exposed the glaring truth that she wasn't perfect after all. She chose to try and live up to the role her mother had given her, even though it was an impossible task and it demanded a lot of sacrifice. Looking back, my friend laments that she never gave herself permission to learn how to do things that were harder for her out of fear that they would expose her imperfection. Instead, she simply walked away from them and gravitated toward those things that came naturally, even if she didn't enjoy them as much.

Do you feel the same pressure to meet other people's expectations? It's so easy to pour time and mental energy into managing our images so that the people in our lives won't be disappointed or disillusioned. However, when we try to live up to what other people want us to be, we often lose ourselves in the process.

In Search of an Answer

So who are you?

That's a question that we all wrestle with in one way or another, and until we can answer it we will seek our identities through things like our jobs, our relationships, our lifestyles, and our performance. If we don't know who we are, we will seek our validation from other broken people, even if that means living up to their unrealistic expectations. So this is no small question; it's foundational to everything that we do. If we could somehow answer this question once and for all, then we could stop looking to other people to answer it for us. We could stop trying to live up to ever-shifting standards of success that society sets for us - a bar that seems to be just a little higher than we are able to jump.

However, we cannot answer this question on our own. After all, we are just as prone to place unrealistic expectations on ourselves. Plus, the natural tendency is to build our identities upon the ever-shifting sands of social norms, rather than upon the bedrock of truth. When we do this, we put ourselves in danger of having our self-images come crashing down around us. When the standards that we use to prove our worth are continually moving, we can never rest; we will constantly need to shore up the foundations of our identities.

Thankfully, there's an alternative. You see, despite what society might tell us, we are not self-made men and women. We have a Creator who made us, and He made us for a purpose. Therefore, rather than attempt to prove our worth and earn our identities through our own efforts, we can go to our Creator and <u>ask Him</u> to show us who we are and the purposes for which He created us. We can allow Him to answer the question.

Self-Love Isn't the Problem

Some people might balk at the need to ask God who we are and why we're valuable. After all, don't we already think too highly of ourselves as it is? Admittedly, we do live in an increasingly self-focused culture. Sociologists claim that this is the single most narcissistic time in history. It is the age of instant-access social media, where we can keep our "friends" updated on what we're doing, what we're eating, and what we're thinking. We don't even think twice about it. <u>Paul warned his protégée</u> Timothy that in the last days, "people would become lovers of themselves" (2 Timothy 3:2 NIV).[1] Sadly, this is increasingly becoming the norm. So why do we even need to talk about who we are and what our purpose is? Doesn't that just perpetuate the problem?

Not at all! You see, the real issue is not loving ourselves too much; rather, it's trying to love ourselves for the wrong reasons. After all, God loves us and so should we. But far too many of us are walking around with a warped misperception of what makes us worthy of love.

When we don't know who we are, when we aren't secure in who God made us to be, then we will naturally look to other people and things to define us. I, for one, have spent way too much of my life thinking that my value was determined by things like my grades, the group of people I hung out with, my social standing, my success in sports, the jobs I got, and the accolades I garnered. I spent far too many years trying to prove my worth to my parents, my peers, my God, and even to myself. I got so fixated on becoming what I thought other people wanted me to be that I lost sight of who I really was.

Then in my early twenties God began to gently expose the misconceptions I had been carrying around regarding my self-image. He began to bring people and books into my life that challenged my warped perceptions of myself. He started to strip away many of the things that I had founded my identity upon, forcing me to run to Him and His word for insight and direction. And He began a decades-long process of reconstructing the way I view myself, which in turn impacted the way I view and interact with other people and with God Himself.

Now, more than twenty years into this journey of discovery, I can honestly say that God has freed me from so many of the chains of insecurity that held me captive. There is nothing more liberating than knowing who I am and what God has created me to do. I want the same thing for you. I want you to understand who you are, so that you can stop looking to other people to tell you who you should be. I want you to know your inherent value, so that you can stop trying to prove your worth day in and day out. I want you to know just how deeply your Creator loves you, so that you can stop trying to earn love from broken people by any means necessary. And I want you to understand what He has created you to do, so that you can embrace your purpose in life.

That's why I've written this book- to distill two decades worth of wrestling with God regarding my identity, two decades worth of studying His word and applying the truths that I've found there. I am indebted to others who have wrestled with this same question and shared their insights with me, authors like Brennan Manning and John Eldredge and mentors like Mike Erre and Don Springer. These are just a few of the countless voices that God has used to shape my self-image and liberate me from my bondage to insecurity and people pleasing. My prayer is that this book will be one of the voices that God uses to help you in your journey to freedom as well.

So who are you?

If you ever find yourself wrestling with that question, this book is for you. I wrote it for anybody who, like me, has wondered whether their life matters or whether they are becoming the person God created them to be. So whether you think you already know who you are or haven't the slightest clue, I invite you to journey with me through God's word so that our Creator can answer this question for us once and for all.

> *God, show us who we are so that we can stop chasing after moving targets.*
> *Show us who we are so that we can stop looking to broken, insecure people to tell us.*
> *Show us who we are so that we can rest in this truth and live out of who you made us to be.*
> *Show us who we are, I pray. Amen.*

Think About It –

Often when I read a book, I just put my head down and plow through the material. Then, when I get to the end, I close the book, set it back on the shelf and move on. While I may feel a sense of accomplishment in finishing something, my harried pace doesn't allow much space for the truths between the covers to sink in. I'm like the shallow soil in Jesus's parable about the sower, where the seeds have no time to put down roots, so they quickly wither and die. Yet, I suspect you're not reading this just for information; you want genuine transformation. And in order to get that, you actually need to create space for the seeds of truth to put down roots in your life. So at the end of each chapter I'm going to include a few questions to get you to stop and wrestle with the ideas we have just examined. I encourage you to take the time to engage these questions. Write your answers in the space provided or in a journal.

* Who do you think you are? What words would you use to define yourself?

- What sort of things do you tend to base your identity upon: Your accomplishments? Your failures? Comments people have made about you?

- How do these things shape the way you view yourself?

- How do they shape the way you interact with God and others?

CHAPTER 2

Created With a Purpose

You were made by God and for God
and until you understand that,
life will never make sense.
– Rick Warren

I don't often cry when I watch movies. My wife tears up during a commercial, but it takes something special to get my waterworks going. That said, I admit that I shed more than a few tears while watching the final installment of the *Lord of the Rings* trilogy, *The Return of the King.*

Toward the end of the movie, Aragorn, one of the central characters in the story, is crowned King of Gondor, one of the largest and most influential kingdoms of Middle Earth, and a throng of important looking people are there to celebrate the joyful day. As King Aragorn and his bride make their way through the multitude of onlookers, he comes to the small group of hobbits who have played such an integral role in the events that led to that point. These four hobbits look like children standing in a sea of adults, noticeable only because of their small stature and the plainness of their clothing amidst the splendor of the crowd. As Aragorn approaches, the hobbits begin to bow, but he stops them unexpectedly and declares, "No my friends, you bow to no one."

Then, the King kneels down before them, showing his respect and appreciation for all that they had accomplished. The hobbits can only stand there with open mouthed amazement as the rest of the gathered onlookers follow the King's lead, kneeling in tribute to them.

That's when I lose it. I can't help it; there's just something about watching a great man publicly acknowledge his respect for these seemingly insignificant little guys that connects deeply with a yearning within me, a yearning to be recognized and respected by those whose opinions matter most. I suppose it is a yearning for significance.

As a pastor, I have come to realize that most people carry within their hearts a similar yearning. Most people want to know that their presence in this world matters, that they matter. I can already see this yearning in my boys, the way they look over after hitting a baseball or making a basket to see if I was watching; to see if their daddy is proud of them.

My boys are too young to watch *The Lord of the Rings* at this point, but I can't wait to share it with them. It's one of those rare trilogies where the last film is the best one, a fitting grand finale. And while I might be tempted to jump right to the last installment, I would never do so, because it would rob them of the richness of the story. The first two movies provide a narrative foundation that the final one is built upon, a context that is imperative if they are going to appreciate the outcome as much as their dad did. Therefore, when the time comes to introduce my boys to Middle Earth and the quest to destroy the One Ring, I will start at the beginning.

In the same way, in a book about identity we might be tempted to jump right to the conclusion, to demand a quick answer to our questions so that we can go back to our regularly scheduled lives. But answers without the underlying context is like eating dessert without dinner. It may be momentarily satisfying, but it is insubstantial and ultimately detrimental to our health. Therefore, if we are going to wrestle with the question of who we are, we need to start at the beginning, back when God first designed us, and examine what He created us for in the first place.

The Genesis of Man

Mankind is not an accident. We cannot trace our origin from some bacteria that just happened to spring into existence billions of years ago; we are not the unintentional product of countless random mutations. We were intentionally created with a specific purpose in mind. The Bible is clear on that. The question is, what purpose did our Creator have in mind when He formed us?

To answer that, we must first ask the question, "Why did God create at all?" Was He somehow incomplete? A quick survey of scripture suggests that the answer to that question is a resounding, No! The Author of Life is not deficient in any way, nor is He dependent upon His creation for anything. The Apostle Paul declared that "The God who made the world and everything in it ... is not served by human hands, as if he needed anything" (Acts 17:24-25). Furthermore, He did not need us because He was lonely. Our triune God already had community in and of Himself: Father, Son and Spirit. Nor did He create out of some innate sense of insecurity. It's not like he needed His creation to stroke His ego or give Him purpose.

God didn't need His creation to complete Him. In fact, He didn't need to create at all, but He chose to anyway. Why?

I would suggest that the best answer is simply that He wanted to, because it brought Him pleasure. Poets write poems and artists create works of art to express themselves. Likewise, God created the universe and everything in it as an expression of God Himself, a reflection of His glory.[2] The opening chapters of the Bible paint a picture of God as a divine artist. He begins by calling the raw materials into existence *ex nihlo* – from nothing. And then He begins to impose order and reason. He separates the light from the darkness, creating day and night. He makes boundaries for the waters so that there will be dry land, sea and sky. Then He begins to fill the air with birds, the seas with fish and the land with animals. And all throughout this creation process, the Architect of the Universe steps back and admires His work, declaring over and again, "It is good!"

Then, on the sixth and final day of creation God makes mankind. Some theologians have pointed to the fact that mankind was created last as an indicator of our special status; they suggest that we were God's best and final work. By that same argument, one could contend that women are the cream of God's creative crop, since Eve was made after Adam. There's probably something to that, but that's another conversation.

However, we don't need to look to the order of creation for proof of our special status. We simply need to consider the way in which we were made. Over the first five days of creation, God spoke things into existence. By His word, the world was shaped. But when it came to humanity, He got His hands dirty.

In Genesis 2, we read, "the Lord God formed the man from the dust of the ground and breathed into His nostrils the breath of life, and the man became a living being" (Genesis 2:7). Can you picture God kneeling down in the dirt and scraping a pile of dust into the shape of a man? Given how He's approached the rest of the creation process, using words rather than His hands to accomplish His will, it seems unnecessary - but that's how scripture describes it. He forms the first human being out of the dust, and then He leans over this pile of dirt and breathes life into it. Thus was man made, a beautiful synthesis of corruptible flesh and divine spirit.

So the manner in which we were created was unique and intimately personal, but we still haven't answered why He chose to create mankind in the first place.

Made in the Image of God

> Then God said, 'Let us make man in our image, in
> our likeness, and let them rule over the fish of the

sea and the birds of the air, over the livestock, over
all the earth, and over all the creatures that move
along the ground. So God created man in His own
image, in the image of God He created him; male
and female He created them. (Genesis 1:26-27)

Growing up, my image of God was influenced by *The Far Side* comic
strips that I read. In one of them, God is pictured as a wizened
old man with a flowing white beard and a bushy white unibrow,
cooking up the world in His kitchen like He was baking a cake. As
silly as it may sound, when I thought about the image of God, this
was the picture that percolated up in my mind. So when I read that
we were made in God's image, I figured He just made us to look
like Him, minus the prominent facial hair.

However, when this passage says that mankind has been made
"in the image of God," it is almost certainly not talking about physical
attributes. After all, Jesus declared that "God is spirit" (John 4:24),
not flesh. God the Father does not necessarily have a physical body,
let alone a flowing white beard and unibrow. Furthermore, the
author of Genesis points out that both male and female have been
made in His image, so to interpret this passage in strictly physical
terms would leave us with some confusing questions about God: Is
God male or female? Is He only one or the other, or a synthesis of
both? Does He have more masculine or feminine traits? You get the
picture. It is unlikely that the "image of God" has anything to do
with our physical bodies, and to interpret it in that way would be us
attempting to make God in our image, not the other way around.

If that's not what this passage means, then what is the author
of Genesis suggesting when he declares that we are made in God's
image? A number of scholars and theologians throughout the
centuries have suggested that it has more to do with character
traits than physical traits.

The fact is we do resemble our Creator in a lot of ways: we, like
our God, have the ability to create and to reason. Furthermore,

He designed us to be in community, just as He is in community with Himself- Father, Son and Spirit. Plus, we each possess a soul, an eternal spark within our finite bodies. The list could go on, but even if we were to compile an exhaustive list of ways in which we resemble our Creator, we would still be left with the question of why He would want us to resemble Him. What was the goal of creating image-bearers in the first place?

Royal Representatives

In the ancient Near East, kings often ruled over sprawling kingdoms. In those days, they obviously did not have cell phones, email or video conferencing; nor did they have access to motor vehicles or airplanes. News only traveled at the speed of the quickest horse, so communicating instructions from one side of a kingdom to the other could often take weeks or even months. Therefore, kings appointed emissaries to represent them throughout their kingdom.

These ambassadors were not kings; they had no right to rule in and of themselves. But the rightful ruler of the land had chosen them to be his representatives, so they governed with the full authority of the king. Therefore, because of the authority that had been bestowed upon these royal representatives, their commands were law; they were treated with all the honor and respect due the king. Furthermore, to mistreat or disrespect one of these emissaries was equivalent to mistreating or disrespecting the king himself.

In the same way, God created mankind in His image in order to be His representatives to the world that He created. God said, "Let us make man in our image, in our likeness, and *let them rule* over the fish of the sea and the birds of the air, over the livestock, over all the earth, and over all the creatures that move along the ground" (Genesis 1:26, emphasis added). Did you get that? Our being created in His image is tied to the call to rule in His name.

God is the sovereign owner of the universe; He made it and it belongs to Him. However, He entrusted the responsibility of caring for the world and everything in it to mankind. Adam and Eve, our most ancient ancestors, were created in His image in order to be His representatives, living in and caring for the world He had made. They never earned the right to rule; rather, this authority was bestowed upon them by the rightful owner, the King of Creation.

In short, being made in God's image has more to do with our purpose than it does with any particular attribute. Certainly we carry within us similarities to our creator, but at the end of the day the purpose for our creation was to represent Him and to rule in His name.

Created for Communion

Unlike human kings, who are unable to govern every part of their kingdom at once, our Sovereign God is not limited by time and space. He holds the universe in the palm of His hand, yet knows the movement of every particle within the smallest drop of water. He did not need humanity to take care of His creation; He could have easily done it Himself. Yet, He still chose to entrust dominion to us. He chose to place our earliest ancestors in the Garden of Eden to "work it and take care of it" (Genesis 2:15) and He chose to allow Adam to name the animals, an act that established mankind's place over the rest of God's creatures. So despite the fact that He did not need our help, God chose to entrust His creation to mankind. However, He never intended for us to rule alone.

We were created for community, both with God and with one another.

In the opening chapters of Genesis, we see God actively participating in Adam and Eve's lives. He instructs them how to live in this paradise He had created, shows them what to eat and what to avoid. He leads each animal before Adam to be named. And He takes walks in the Garden, no doubt interacting with His chosen representatives while enjoying His creation. Although God transcends time and space, He was no absentee landlord. He was intimately involved in the first-couple's lives, and that's the way He intended it.

Furthermore, He designed us to live in communion with one another. The very first thing that God declared to be deficient in His creation was the fact that Adam was alone (Genesis 2:18). So when none of the animals were found to be suitable partners, God took a part of Adam's side and fashioned Eve to be his helper and counterpart.[3] She, like Adam, was created in God's image and tasked with ruling over creation alongside her husband. Together, they were capable of fulfilling God's mandate to be fruitful and multiply and to take dominion over the world.

As Genesis 2 comes to a close, we are left with a beautiful picture of intimacy. Adam and Eve are together in the Garden, naked and vulnerable before one another and God, and yet they feel absolutely no shame. This was the way God intended us to live. Sadly, this perfect state of innocence did not last long.

Think About It –

Read the creation account recorded in Genesis 1–2. Then answer the questions below.

• What stands out to you about the way God created man as opposed to the other creatures?

• What is significant about the fact that mankind was created "in God's image?"

• For what purpose did God create humanity? (see Genesis 1:26-27)

CHAPTER 3

Fear and Fig Leaves

We can easily forgive a child who is afraid of the dark;
the real tragedy of life is when men are afraid of the light.
- Plato

When my wife and I were preparing to bring our first son, Ethan, home from the hospital, we tried to root out anything in our home that could hurt him. We sold our old coffee table with the sharp edges and replaced it with a soft ottoman. We put plug protectors into all the electrical outlets, and latches on all of the cupboard doors. It worked for a while, but then he started crawling and suddenly we realized what rookies we were at baby-proofing a house.

That boy was a prodigy at finding danger. I once found him sucking on a plug protector like it was a pacifier. I figured someone had left it sitting on the floor, so I dried it off and put it back in the outlet. Then I watched as my son used his chubby little fingers to pry it back out of the socket so he could shove it back into his mouth. I knew then that we were in trouble. He could climb long before he could walk. I'd turn my back for a moment and he would be up on the dining room table. And child-protective locks were a game for him. From time to time, I would find Ethan sitting in the kitchen, holding the lock that we had put on the cupboard that held the cleaning products. I had trouble getting that lock open, but to him it was child's play.

As parents of infants, we do everything we can to protect our kids, but as they grow older, our job shifts from removing every dangerous object to teaching them how to avoid hurting themselves. After all, we cannot go everywhere with them and watch over them every second of the day. Even if we could, that kind of hovering would only stunt their maturation process and leave them dependent upon us for everything. So rather than remove the kitchen stove, which has the potential to burn curious hands, we teach our children about the dangers of fire. Sadly, more often than not, the real lesson comes when they singe a finger or two.

Similarly, when God, our Father was designing the world, He had to choose whether or not to protect His image-bearers from anything that could potentially hurt them. He could have created a paradise that was free from danger, a world that was sanitized and safe, where the only decision Adam and Eve needed to make was from which tree they were going to get their next meal. But God was not interested in raising full-grown infants who had to be coddled and spoon fed; He wanted emotionally mature men and women who had the capacity to make decisions. He wanted responsible representatives who were capable of faithfully caring for His creation. Therefore, He decided not to shelter them from hard choices.

The Cost of Love

One of the most curious parts of the creation narrative is found in Genesis 2:16. God has just created the first man and placed him in the Garden of Eden. And then He tells Adam, "You are free to eat from any tree in the garden; but you must not eat from the tree of knowledge of good and evil, for when you eat from it you will certainly die." It has always struck me as a bit odd that God would intentionally design the garden with something that was

20

off limits. He could have just as easily placed Adam in Eden and said: "Everything is fair game, so have fun and I'll see you later this evening for our walk."

Why would God create the tree with the forbidden fruit in the first place? After all, He is omniscient; He knows the end from the beginning.[4] God must have known the damage that this tree would cause; He must have foreseen the part it would play in the Fall. Yet, He chose to create the tree anyway. Why make something that had the potential to wreak such havoc and cause so much pain?

Believe it or not, He did it as an act of love. Allow me to explain.

Imagine for a moment that I could build a computer and then program it so that every time I log in, it would declare, "Good morning, Eric. I love you." Would you say that this computer truly loves me? Of course not! It has neither the ability to love me nor to hate me; all it can do is obey its programming.

Now consider my son Ethan. When my boy says he loves me, it warms my heart. Why? Because he could just as easily say, "Go away daddy, I want mommy."

You see, a key component to a genuine relationship is that both parties must have the ability to choose not to be in relationship. Since a computer can't refuse to do my bidding, the fact that it does what I want it to do doesn't mean much. But the fact that my boy can choose to push me away makes the times that he moves toward me that much more meaningful. The fact that he can, and often does, disobey makes it that much more satisfying when he trusts my leadership and obeys my directions. Freewill makes meaningful relationship possible.

By the way, this is the same answer that I give to those who ask, "If God is really all-powerful and He created the universe, then how can we account for evil in His good creation?" It's because He chose to design mankind with the ability to obey or disobey Him, the ability to move toward Him or to run from Him.

CS Lewis put it this way in his book *Mere Christianity*:

> If a thing is free to be good it is also free to be bad. And freewill is what has made evil possible. Why, then, did God give them freewill? Because freewill, though it makes evil possible, is also the only thing that makes possible any love or goodness or joy worth having. A world of automata – of creatures that worked like machines – would hardly be worth creating... Of course God knew what would happen if they used their freedom the wrong way: apparently he thought it worth the risk.[5]

So why did God place that tree in the center of the garden and then call it off limits? He did it because He wanted His human representatives to have a choice: trust and obey His commands or reject Him as their sovereign King. He could have designed mankind without freewill. No doubt there would be a lot less pain and suffering in the world if He had, but a world without pain would also be a world without love. It would be a world full of robots going through our programming, but lacking any ability to have a relationship with our Creator or with one another.

In short, God gave mankind free will; He gave us the ability to freely choose whether or not to trust Him and walk in intimate relationship with Him. Unfortunately, or perhaps inevitably, our most ancient forbearers chose to disobey and, as we will see, that choice has had radical reverberations that affect us to this day.

The Introduction of a New Voice

At the end of Genesis 2, we get a glimpse of the world as our Creator intended it. Adam and Eve are together in the Garden, naked and vulnerable before God and one another, yet neither of them feels shame or fear due to their nakedness. They simply are as God created them to be. Sadly, the world as they knew it was about to change.

You see, up to this point Adam and Eve had no reason to question God's goodness or doubt His trustworthiness. He was their Creator and they trusted Him implicitly. Then all of a sudden there is a new voice that forces its way into their lives; Satan comes slithering into the picture and begins to sow seeds of doubt. He begins by questioning the single limitation that God had given them: "Did God really say, 'You must not eat from any tree in the garden?'" (Genesis 3:1)

Of course God had not prohibited Adam and Eve from eating of every tree, just one of them. And Eve is quick to correct him: "We may eat fruit from the trees in the garden, but God did say, 'You must not eat fruit from the tree that is in the middle of the garden, and you must not touch it⁶, or you will die'" (Genesis 3:2).

Satan quickly challenges God's warning: "You will not certainly die…For God knows that when you eat from it your eyes will be opened, and you will be like God, knowing good and evil" (Genesis 3:4-5).

What I find so fascinating about this interaction is the way in which Satan entices Adam and Eve to sin. He doesn't just hold up a piece of the forbidden fruit and encourage them to take a bite. Rather, he begins by undermining their perception of God. He calls God's trustworthiness and goodness into question, suggesting that their Creator is lying to them, that He is holding out on them. Satan starts here because he knows that once the first-couple begins to question whether God is really trustworthy, whether He really has their best interest in mind, then suddenly the fruit will begin to look a whole lot more enticing.

What we see happening in the Garden of Eden is a moral and spiritual descent into sin that every one of us has experienced in one fashion or another. This descent into sin does not usually begin with the sinful act or even with temptation. Rather, it starts when we begin to question God:

"Is God really trustworthy?"

"Is He holding out on me?"

"Does He see what I'm going through?"

"Does He even care?"

When we begin to question God's goodness and trustworthiness, our natural impulse is to take care of ourselves by running to other created things. We begin to look to *pseudo saviors*- anything which we believe can give us what we want or can save us from what we fear the most.

For instance, if we fear rejection, we may run to the pseudo savior of attractiveness; We may hyper-fixate on the food we eat, on physical fitness and on dressing the right way in order to ensure our acceptance from others. Or if we fear the unexpected loss of control, we might run to the pseudo savior of money, which we believe can help us overcome any unforeseen calamity we encounter. We might fixate on accumulating a large bank account, or holding onto every penny like Ebenezer Scrooge. Whatever our fear may be, if we begin to doubt God's trustworthiness, then there are a slew of pseudo saviors waiting in the wings, promising to provide us with what we want most. Whether they can actually provide what they promise is another story.

In the case of Adam and Eve, they began to fear that God had been holding out on them, that He had intentionally left something out when He designed them. Even though they had no concept of good and evil, they suddenly felt deficient without it. So they took matters into their own hands. They disobeyed God and ate the very fruit which He told them to avoid. Unfortunately, they were unprepared for what their disobedience would introduce into their lives.

Casualties of the Fall –

> When the woman saw that the fruit of the tree was good for food and pleasing to the eye, and also desirable for gaining wisdom, she took some and ate it. She also gave some to her husband, who

was with her, and he ate it. Then the eyes of both
of them were opened, and they realized they were
naked; so they sewed fig leaves together and made
coverings for themselves. (Genesis 3:6-7)

As soon as they ate the fruit, they "realized" they were naked.

Doesn't that strike you as a bit odd? Were Adam and Eve blind
to the fact that they didn't have any clothing on prior to this? Of
course not! It's just that now, in the aftermath of their disobedience,
shame and guilt have entered into God's good creation and begun
to wreak havoc. And the first casualty of the Fall is their self-image.

Sin did not change Adam and Eve's inherent value. They still
bore the indelible fingerprints of the Creator, still reflected His
image, but sin warped their perceptions of themselves like one of
those misshapen carnival mirrors. Rather than see themselves as
they really were, all they could see was the distorted image that sin
reflected back to them, and for the first time in history, mankind
felt insecure.

The scene plays out like that nightmare where you are standing
on stage, delivering a speech when all of a sudden you realize you
are in your underwear. In that moment, the speech is forgotten,
replaced by a crushing sense of embarrassment and vulnerability.
In the same way, prior to the Fall, Adam and Eve had felt secure
in their identity, comfortable with being unclothed because they
had nothing to hide; but suddenly they became aware of their
nakedness, aware that they were exposed and vulnerable, and they
were ashamed.

Their feelings of inadequacy and insecurity lead to the second
casualty of the Fall – their intimacy with one another. You see, God
designed mankind to be naked and unashamed. That does not mean
we are supposed to be nudists; rather, He intended for us to be fully
known. As His representatives, we were made to be completely
open and vulnerable with Him and with each other; however, due
to the distorting effects that sin has on our self-image, we have an

innate aversion to vulnerability. We seek to cover it up, to hide our real selves from God and others. Why? Because deep down we fear that if people see us for who we really are, they will reject us.

So, rather than being exposed and vulnerable, we hide. We hide our true selves behind false veneers and then hope that nobody notices. For Adam and Eve, they reached for the closest thing at hand to mask their naked vulnerability – fig leaves. We have had a lot more time to come up with more subtle coverings, some of which we will explore in the next chapter.

Sin's distorting effects not only caused them to hide from one another, but from God as well. After hiding their vulnerability behind a layer of fig leaves, they heard God coming through the garden and a feeling that they had never experienced before griped their heart - guilt. They were suddenly overcome with guilt because of their disobedience, and their fight-or-flight instinct kicked in.

"Then the man and his wife heard the sound of the Lord God as he was walking in the garden in the cool of the day, *and they hid from the Lord God* among the trees of the garden" (Genesis 3:8, emphasis added).

The scene would be comical if it wasn't so tragic. God's self-appointed representatives, His image-bearers are draped in fig leaves and huddling behind a tree, hiding from the all-knowing creator and sustainer of the universe. Their reaction reminds me of the way my childhood dog, Heidi, reacted whenever she got in the trash. We would walk into the house and, rather than greeting us at the door with eager tongue and wagging tail, she would slink off with her head hung low. We didn't need to see the trash scattered around the kitchen to know that she'd done something wrong; her body language declared her guilt. In the same way, rather than being joyful to hear their creator coming as they always had been before, Adam and Eve crept off into the shadows with their tails between their legs.

I have no doubt that God already knew what had happened

and was aware of the unholy contagion that had been introduced into His creation. But, like a parent who wants His children to take ownership of their actions, He led with a question rather than an accusation.

God called to them, "Where are you?"

Adam, probably recognizing the futility of hiding from Him, chose to answer from the shadows: "I heard you in the garden, and I was afraid because I was naked; so I hid" (Genesis 3:10).

Why was Adam afraid? Not because he'd disobeyed, at least not overtly. No, he admits that he was afraid because he was naked, because he was exposed and vulnerable. Sin had corrupted our oldest ancestor's self-perception, warped it into something he was ashamed of, and he was suddenly terrified that God would see him the way he saw himself. So he ran into the shadows and hid.

Furthermore, when God comes right out and asks him whether he'd eaten fruit from the forbidden tree, Adam doesn't take responsibility for his actions. Instead, he tries to shift the blame: "The woman you put here with me—she gave me some fruit from the tree, and I ate it" (3:12)

Did you catch that? Not only was he trying to throw his wife under the bus to save his skin, he even tries to shift some of the blame onto God for creating Eve in the first place. Adam was employing the "don't blame me" method of self-preservation. "Don't blame me that I blatantly disobeyed a direct command from you. You made her, and she made me do it. I'm just a victim in all of this."

For her part, Eve doesn't do much better. As soon as God turns toward her, she points at the serpent and declares, "He deceived me, and that's why I ate the fruit."

Sadly, when we feel insecure and under attack, it's usually easier to point somewhere else and pass the blame than it is to take ownership for our choices and accept the repercussions. In the end, despite all their excuses, the first-couple are unable to avoid the consequences of their actions.

Merciful Curses

Since Adam and Eve had blatantly disobeyed God's one and only command, God lays out some repercussions for all the parties involved.

First, He cursed the serpent, the instigator who tempted Adam and Eve to question God's goodness and encouraged them to take matters into their own hands.[7]

He then turns to Adam and Eve and hands down what, at first glance, seem to be some pretty harsh punishments. To Eve and all women after her, He curses the act of childbearing, increasing the pain with which women would give birth. Interestingly, this curse corresponds with the very first commandment that God gave to Adam and Eve: "Be fruitful and multiply" (Genesis 1:22). In effect, He was frustrating the very thing that He'd called women to do.

He also curses Eve's relationship with her husband, turning it from a mutually harmonious relationship into a veritable power struggle.[8]

And for Adam and all men after him, God curses the work of his hands. It is not that work is a product of the Fall; God actually designed us to work, having placed Adam in the garden "to work it and take care of it" (Genesis 2:15). However, as a result of God's curse, work becomes laborious and mankind finds themselves relegated to a lifetime of toil and hardship.

Now, we might read these curses and get the impression that God is just punishing them for their disobedience. You might be thinking, "All this for one little piece of fruit?! What a harsh response!" However, even while he disciplined his wayward children, God was still pursuing relationship with them and us. You see, our Creator knew that now that sin and death had entered the world, humanity was fundamentally warped. No longer would our tendency be to seek God on our own; rather, we would naturally gravitate toward self-sufficiency. Adam and Eve had already revealed mankind's propensity toward taking matters into our own hands. So God took drastic action. He frustrated the very things that both men and women normally rely on to find their identity and fulfillment. He did it so that we would be driven back into His arms.

For the woman, he frustrated her identity as a mother and as a wife.

For the man, he frustrated the work of his hands.

No longer can our relationships with our spouse or our children complete us. No longer can we find total fulfillment through our jobs. By cursing the very things that men and women typically look to for identity and fulfillment, our Creator cut out a God-shaped hole in each and every one of us. While we may try to fill this hole with any number of other things, we can never be fully satisfied apart from Him. Looked at from this perspective, we can begin to see the curses for what they were: the merciful discipline of a loving father. They were His way of turning our wandering hearts back toward Him, because at the end of the day, His greatest desire is relationship with us. So, like a good parent, His discipline was redemptive, not simply punitive.[9]

Through God's response, He showed Himself to be both just and merciful. He is just, because He was unwilling to simply turn a blind eye to their sins. Yet at the same time, He showed mercy to His wayward children. He did not destroy them, but rather disciplined them with the hope of leading them back into relationship with Him.

And He wasn't finished. As Genesis 3 comes to a close, God did for Adam and Eve what they had ineffectually tried to do for themselves – he covered their naked vulnerability.

First Blood

When Adam and Eve realized they were naked, they grabbed the closest thing at hand to try and cover themselves. But their fig-leaf coverings wouldn't last. They were a temporary fix. God had a more enduring solution in mind. In Genesis 3:21, we read that "the LORD God made garments of skin for Adam and his wife and clothed them." Have you ever thought about where those skins came from?

Obviously, God had to kill an animal to provide the skins that would cover them. This would be the first recorded death in God's good creation, and this creature died as a direct result of Adam and Eve's sin. It's interesting that God would choose to do this, especially since the shame they felt about their nakedness was a direct result of their disobedience. However, time and again God's actions show that He isn't interested in simply punishing His people every time they mess up. Our Father in Heaven is all about redemption; He is all about restoring mankind to the dignity He created us to possess. This first death was a precursor to the entire sacrificial system that He would introduce when He created the nation of Israel to be His representatives. Furthermore, it foreshadowed an even greater redemptive act, one that would affect all of mankind.

One day, God's one and only son, Jesus the Christ, would take on human flesh and die to permanently cover our nakedness. The fig leaves were a hastily conceived covering, the skins God provided were only somewhat longer lasting, but through Jesus' sacrifice, God would deal with the problem that sin introduced into His good creation once and for all.

Corrupted Images

Genesis 3 is one of the saddest chapters in human history. God had created Adam and Eve for a unique and significant purpose: they were intended to act as His chosen representatives, bearing His image and ruling over His creation. Plus, He intended for them to rule in intimate communion with both Himself and with one another. Unfortunately, the moment another voice spoke up and questioned His trustworthiness, God's representatives rebelled and disobeyed the one and only stipulation He'd laid out for them.

Through their disobedience, sin entered the world, warping and corrupting it. Shame distorted their self-image and drove them into hiding, both from God and from one another. In the end, God was forced to frustrate creation even more, altering the very things that His representatives would normally find joy and satisfaction in, so that they would ultimately be driven back into His arms. And He made provision so that one day, His children would no longer be shackled by sin and would no longer see themselves through the distorted reflection of the Fall.

Jesus died to redeem us from the corrupting influence of sin, His death on the cross doing what no amount of fig leaves ever could. Sadly, some two-thousand years after Jesus paid the ultimate price, we still question God's goodness and struggle with the consequences of the Fall. We still see ourselves through the distorted lens of our sin and hide our true selves from God and one another for fear that we will be weighed, measured and found wanting. In the next few chapters, we will examine some of the ways in which the Fall still impacts our lives and warps everything from our self-image to our relationships.

Think About It –

•   Why did God create mankind with free will?

•   Given the damage our free will has caused, what does that say about how much God values authentic relationship with us?

•   When we begin to question God's trustworthiness, our natural impulse is to look to *pseudo saviors* - anything which we believe can give us what we want or can save us from what we fear the most. Adam and Eve looked to the forbidden fruit to help them overcome a perceived deficiency in their design, and they reached for fig leaves to cover their nakedness. What sort of pseudo saviors do you find yourself running to again and again?

- What are you hoping these pseudo saviors will save you from?

- How did sin warp Adam and Eve's perception of themselves?

- How did it affect their relationship with God and with one another?

- In what ways were the curses redemptive?

- What do they reveal about God's view of us in spite of our sin?

CHAPTER 4

Hypocrites

All the world's a stage, And all the men and women merely players.
- William Shakespeare, *As You Like It*

Recently, a friend of mine asked me to dress up as Santa Claus for a community Christmas party. I had already said yes before I considered the fact that I was missing just about every quality you look for in a good fake Santa: White hair and beard? Nope. Round face with rosy cheeks? Not really. Gut like a bowl full of jelly? Not even close. I was going to be a sorry excuse for Saint Nicolas. No problem, my friend assured me. Nothing a wig, a beard and a few pillows couldn't fix.

I had my doubts as I pulled on the Santa costume, strapped on the beard and climbed up into the fire engine that was to be my sleigh for the night. But as soon as the siren started blaring and I saw the excitement in the children's faces as we pulled into the parking lot, I swallowed my worries and channeled my jolly inner fat-man. It was show time!

I have to admit, being Santa was pretty fun. Everywhere I looked, I saw smiling faces and kids quaking with eagerness to talk with me. Plus, I got credit for all the presents parents were going to have to pay for. The two hours I spent on the Santa-throne flew by and before I knew it I was out of costume and back into my street clothes.

However, after the excitement of being Santa, I didn't really anticipate how odd it would feel to go somewhere without the costume. As I walked back through the party, everything seemed different. The lights didn't seem to sparkle quite as brightly, the fake snow on the ground didn't look as convincing, and the crowds didn't smile at me like they had just a few minutes before. After all the attention I'd just experienced as Santa, I kind of felt invisible. It was a bit of a letdown, and I was tempted to run back in and throw on the costume for one more hit of Christmas cheer.

That evening, I learned how intoxicating it can be to slip on a mask and pretend to be someone else. It gives you a freedom to let loose a little, to ham it up without fear that everything you say can and will be used against you in the court of public opinion. For one brief hour, I was free to look people in the eye and smile without worrying that they wouldn't smile back or might think I was being too forward. I liked the feeling, and I secretly wished I could wear the costume again.

There is a word for people who wear masks and pretend to be someone they're not – we call them actors.

Performers

In ancient Greece, stage plays were as popular and culturally relevant as blockbuster movies are today. However, unlike Hollywood movies where the camera can zoom in for a close up, Greek stage actors had to figure out some way to communicate emotion to everyone in the amphitheater. One way they did this was through the use of masks. I'm not talking rubber masks like you see on Halloween; these things were big, large enough for the people in the nose-bleed section to be able to tell whether the character was happy or sad, angry or scared.

The use of masks on the stage also meant that it didn't really matter who was wearing them. One actor could play a number of different characters in the same play, and nobody would be the wiser. Sounds like some of the movies Eddie Murphy has cranked out over the last couple decades. I should mention that in those days, stage actors were known by a different name – hypocrites.

The term hypocrite has come to carry a lot of negative connotations. It's often used to label someone who says one thing and does the opposite, or a person who criticizes others for doing something that they do themselves. But originally, the term was simply used to describe someone who wears a mask and plays a role.

In his sermon on the mount, Jesus warned his listeners not to be hypocrites who simply performed for other's attention:

> So when you give to the needy, do not announce it with trumpets, as the hypocrites do in the synagogues and on the streets, to be honored by others...And when you pray, do not be like the hypocrites, for they love to pray standing in the synagogues and on the street corners to be seen by others. Truly I tell you, they have received their reward in full. (Matthew 6:2, 5)

Caring for the needy and prayer are both important aspects of a healthy Christian walk; however, Jesus's warning focuses on the underlying motivations that drive our actions, not the actions themselves. If our generosity or devotion is driven by a desire for public attention and approval, then we have already received our reward, albeit a hollow and fleeting one. Empty religious activity, no matter how well we do it, is just that – empty. It is like wax fruit; it might look attractive and nourishing, but it is devoid of any real spiritual value, especially since our goal is to garner the approval of our peers rather than the approval of our Father in Heaven.

Religious posturing is just one of the many masks that we

might put on in our efforts to hide our inadequacies and win the approval of others.

Modern Day Fig Leaves

As we saw with Adam and Eve in the Garden, once sin had entered creation and begun to exert its corrupting influence, the first casualty was their self-image. Though they bore the indelible fingerprints of the Creator, sin warped their perception of themselves and left them filled with shame. As a result, although they had always been naked and vulnerable, suddenly that vulnerability was terrifying. So they sought to rectify the problem by hiding their nakedness behind a veneer of fig leaves.

Today, we are still plagued by the effects of the Fall. We still carry around chronic feelings of inadequacy that drive us into hiding. However, unlike Adam and Eve, we have known these feelings for most of our lives and have had a lot longer to come up with better, more subtle coverings for ourselves. We have become experts at hiding our nakedness and covering our imperfections. Yet, the purpose of these modern coverings is the same as the fig-leaf garments that Adam and Eve made for themselves - they protect us from being exposed and vulnerable to rejection.

Let's take a look at a few of these modern-day masks that we wear.

Hiding Behind a Smile

Have you ever had one of those Sunday mornings where everything just seems to go wrong? You hit the snooze button one too many times, the kids are crazy, and you and your sweetie are at one another's throats. On the drive to church, you feel like you're in the middle of an angry beehive and you're tempted to turn the car around and go home. But as soon as you get to the church and pile out of the car, your entire countenance changes. You slap a smile over your frustration, put an arm around your spouse and force out a "good morning" to everyone you see.

It's laughable, but for most of us this is an all-too-common occurrence. Regardless of how we are really doing, we wear a smile and pretend to be ok. When a friend asks how we are, we just smile and give a little white lie: "Good" we say, because we figure they don't really want to know the truth and it would be rude of us to impose it on them. Most of the time we can get away with it, because people don't tend to push past the surface level to see whether appearances reflect reality. So we hide behind our smile and pretend that everything is fine.

We have been created for true community, but we often settle for casual relationships and superficial talk about things that don't really matter, because it allows us to maintain our privacy. We may be struggling with addiction, with depression, or with doubts about our faith; maybe we just feel bland. But we are not about to tell others the truth. They might think less of us. So we make small talk, because talking about the weather and sports is a lot safer than sharing what's really going on in our lives. We just drift through life, wearing a fake smile over the carnage of our lives. And since nobody knows what's really going on, nobody can help.

The Mask of Accomplishment

Winston Churchill is one of those men whose name and accomplishments echo long after his death. Yet, like any of us, he suffered from the primal question, "Am I enough?" Though he often seemed unflappable, even in the face of criticism, history has handed us at least one glimpse of the insecurity that lay beneath his confident exterior.

On November 6, 1924, at the age of 50, Churchill became the Chancellor of the Exchequer, one of the most powerful positions in the British government. Though he had been in British politics for years and held a number of important positions, this one was special. It was an office that his father, Lord Randolph Churchill, held when Winston was a boy. In fact, Winston's father had been so preoccupied with his role in the British government that he'd had little time to spend with his son.

During the appointment ceremony, Churchill was to be cloaked in an official robe of his new position. However, when the ceremonial robe was presented to him, Winston waved it off and said, "No, I've brought my own." He then turned to his assistant, who carried a box containing the same robe his father had worn when he had been made Chancellor. As Winston wrapped himself in his father's old robe, he turned to his assistant and said, "Now, maybe I've done something my father would have been proud of."

It is amazing to think that this influential man, a leader of one of the most powerful nations in the world, was still haunted by the question: "Am I enough?" And as he stood in his dad's dusty robe, he hoped that this new accomplishment would prove his worth, both to himself and to his father who had been dead for over twenty-four years.

How many of us are haunted by the question, "Am I enough?" We carry it around like a chain around our hearts, holding us back from being all that God intended. And as we look around, we find ourselves trapped by towering walls of expectation. We may have built these walls ourselves, or had them imposed upon us by someone else, but regardless of where they've come from, we live within their shadow. Day in and day out, we sit within these cells of expectation, held down by the chains of our insecurity. However, deep down in our gut, we believe that if we could only scale these walls, if we could only meet or exceed the expectations that loom over us, then we would be free. We figure that the keys to unlock the chains of insecurity can be found at the top of the walls, if only we could climb high enough.

So what do we do? We construct ladders to climb, with each rung consisting of a different achievement. Some of us climb ladders of intellectual pursuit, with rungs made up of educational degrees.

Others of us scale ladders of physical accomplishment, seeking to prove our worth by climbing to the top of the rankings. Still others seek to climb corporate ladders or social ladders. The ladders we climb can take many forms and are usually influenced by the walls of expectation we hope to scale. Sometimes, like Winston, we climb in the shadow of a parent, trying to prove either to them or to ourselves that we are worthy to be their offspring, that we can match or even surpass their success.

So we climb, with an intensity borne out of the need to answer the question, "Am I enough?" We climb with a focused determination to reach the key to the chains of insecurity that hold us down. We climb and climb and climb...but at what cost? At the cost of our families? Our friendships? Our ability to be present and to find joy in the midst of whatever moment we find ourselves? And if our sense of self-confidence is based upon our achievements, based upon how high we climb, what happens when we stumble? What happens when we slip and fall? Or worse, what happens when we reach the top and realize, like so many before us, that we have placed our ladder against the wrong wall because there is no key here!?

The truth is no amount of personal accomplishment can satiate the fear that we don't measure up. We can never climb high enough to silence the question, "Am I enough?" In the end, our efforts are simply a way to appease our fears and mask our insecurity.

Jerry McGuire Syndrome

In the romantic comedy *Jerry McGuire*, the title character has a problem. He is smooth and confident when it comes to working as an agent to famous sports stars, but clueless when it comes to wooing a woman's heart. However, through the course of the movie, he begins to learn how to put words to his feelings. In one particularly memorable exchange, he finally breaks down and exclaims, "You complete me" to the woman who has captured his heart. Cue the sighs from all the ladies in the theater. For years after that movie came out, "You complete me" was part of our cultural jargon. It was brazenly plagiarized in countless hand-written love notes and repeated by love-struck boys as if it was the magic incantation that would melt a girl's heart.

"You complete me." It may seem like a hokey Hallmark statement, but this saying encapsulates a mindset that has put down deep roots into many a romantic heart.

It is the unofficial mantra of every person who has embraced the idea that they are incomplete by themselves, that they lack something that only another person can provide. So, like a hermit crab looking for the perfect shell, they go from relationship to relationship, looking for the one person who can complete them, the one person who can protect them from the feeling that they are deficient on their own. Now, to be certain, we have been created for community, created to do life with others. Even God pointed out that it's not good for us to be alone. But the motivation of the person suffering from *Jerry McGuire Syndrome* goes far deeper than having meaningful relationships. They honestly don't know who they are by themselves, and they are terrified to find out.

People who suffer with this syndrome simply cannot be single. They jump from relationship to relationship, falling madly into infatuation with each new love interest, and just as quickly fall out of it when it's over. When they are between relationships, they are often depressed, anxious and love-hungry. That's why they don't stay single for long, and why they are often willing to date people that don't seem to be a good fit for them. To someone who feels incomplete on their own, even a bad relationship is better than no relationship at all.

Admittedly, the desire to be known and cherished by another is a natural, wonderful aspect of our design; however, for those who suffer from *Jerry McGuire Syndrome*, relationships are just another fig leaf they paste over their vulnerability, a mask that they use to hide their sense of incompleteness. But like any of the masks we are looking at, the solace they find is fleeting and superficial, because the truth is no person can ever complete us, no matter how well they complement us. Only God can do that.

Mask Collectors

One of the inherent promises of the American Dream is that anyone can become a millionaire. And while some people succeed at that endeavor, a far higher percentage of us are living like we are rich, regardless of what our bank account might say. In their bestselling financial book, *The Millionaire Next Door*, Thomas Stanley and William Danko point out that most millionaires don't look anything like what you'd imagine. They don't drive flashy cars, wear designer clothing or live extravagantly. Instead, they live within or even below their means. They often reside in middle class neighborhoods, drive reliable vehicles that they have owned for several years and are not worried about dressing to impress.

Wait a minute! What about all those people driving the flashy cars, living in the sprawling houses and dressed to the nines?! Stanley and Danko suggest that the vast majority of them are actually drowning in debt in order to look like they're living the good life. Like wannabe cattle ranchers, they may wear a big hat, but they've got no cattle.[10]

Sadly, financial statistics tend to support this conclusion. According to a 2017 report from the Federal Reserve, the average American household has $5,700 in credit card debt. That's just the average! If we only looked at households that regularly carry credit card debt month to month, that average jumps to $16,048 per household, and that number isn't even factoring in mortgages, car loans and student loans.[11] In contrast, 69% of Americans admit that they have less than $1,000 in savings and 34% have no savings at all.[12] We truly are a nation addicted to spending money we haven't earned. But why?

The most obvious reason is that we are trying to maintain the appearance of affluence. We try to keep up with our free-spending neighbors, who may have all the toys we want, but also happen to be leveraged to the hilt. We drive our fig-leaves, wear designer fig-leaves, and live in our fig-leaf homes, hoping that they will cover over the emptiness we feel inside. We buy more and more things, filling our homes and garages to overflowing. And when we run out of room, we rent storage units so that we can make space to accumulate more stuff. To borrow the words of David Ramsey, we "spend money we don't have on things we don't need in order to impress people we don't even like."[13]

Manly Masks

I'm a guy, so I'm not very emotional. At least that's the belief I've carried around with me for as long as I can remember. Nobody ever came out and told me that men are supposed to be stoic, though as a kid I was told plenty of times to just "suck it up" when I got physically or emotionally hurt. Sociologists have pointed out that we tend to teach girls how to vocalize their emotions, but we typically dismiss young boys' feelings, sometimes even shaming them when they get emotional. Admittedly, a couple times I've even caught myself telling one of my sons to "be a big boy and stop crying."

As a result, often young boys (and sometimes girls) learn that there are really only two acceptable emotions: anger and apathy. Thus, when we get backed into a corner or we feel vulnerable, we either retreat behind a mask of apathy, declaring to the world that "I don't care," or we blow up and become angry. That has certainly been my response for much of my life; thankfully, God, in His infinite wisdom, had me marry a Marriage and Family Therapist who made it her mission to help me embrace the myriad emotions churning beneath my stoic exterior.

I have come to realize that while blowing up or shrugging it off might seem like strong, masculine responses, they're really just defense mechanisms. Anger and apathy are masks many of us put on in order to avoid actually delving into the vortex of emotions that are swirling under the surface. It's just too overwhelming to try and make sense of our emotions, especially when we haven't learned how to put words to what we're feeling. Plus, it's terrifying to be vulnerable with someone else about what we are really feeling. This is especially true when we have been taught that emotions are weakness and feelings are unmanly. So we take the easy way out: fight or flight, anger or apathy.

Masking Our Own Pain

Now, the masks we've looked at so far are primarily outward focused; we rely on them to hide our insufficiencies and flaws from others. But what happens when those masks are unable to cover over our own feelings of inadequacy? How can we mask the pain of our insecurity and anxiety from ourselves?

When the ache becomes too much to bear, we will often turn to anything that can dull the pain. Some people will turn to mood-altering substances like alcohol, nicotine, marijuana or other drugs to take the edge off. However, our pain-killers can take other, less obvious forms: food, shopping, busyness, video-games, television, pornography, social media, even sleep. I'm sure you could probably add a few things to this list.

I call these painkillers HABITs, because we tend to run to them when we are **h**ungry, **a**ngry, **b**ored, **i**solated or **t**ired. Why then? Because when we are physically or mentally worn down, our feelings of inadequacy are a lot closer to the surface, demanding our attention like a sliver under the skin. Eventually, we will go searching for something to deaden the ache and distract us from the turmoil we are feeling inside. It is in times like this when our guilty pleasures beckon to us from the shadows, promising us a momentary release. The problem is, they don't have the ability to actually deal with those emotions; all they can do is mask our discomfort from ourselves.

****

These are just a handful of the masks we run to in order to cover our nakedness and hide our vulnerability. No doubt we could add quite a few more to this list, but these are some pretty common ones. Sadly, we often wear our masks without much thought as to the repercussions upon ourselves and our relationships.

The Dark Side of Wearing Masks

As a child who grew up watching the original *Star Wars* trilogy, Darth Vader is hands down my favorite movie villain. Maybe it's the fact that he was so powerful and imposing, like an immovable granite monolith. Every time he walked onto the screen, with his shiny helmet, long black cape and mechanical breathing, I couldn't help but feel awed. Even when everything was falling apart, when his plans were foiled yet again by the rebels, Vader's impassive black mask never betrayed even the slightest shred of concern or fear. He was the embodiment of strength.

Which is probably why I had such a hard time stomaching the portrait of the young Anakin Skywalker (Vader's younger self) that was presented in the second *Star Wars* trilogy. As I watched the development of a gifted, young boy (Episode 1) into an insecure, love-struck adolescent (Episode 2), and finally an emotionally and physically shattered man (Episode 3), I couldn't help but adjust my perception of Darth Vader. Now that I knew the depths of emotion that roiled beneath his dark exterior, my awe for the mighty Vader was tempered with a strong dose of compassion for a broken man who hid behind a mask and a light saber. He held the world at arm's length, garnering fearful respect. But I now saw that he wasn't as superhuman as I'd originally thought. A bit of the luster was lost, but at the same time it made him seem far more human.

In the same way, we hide behind masks because they give us a false sense of security. Behind the mask, we can be anyone we want to be, and nobody needs to know about the anxious, broken, insecure person who is huddled beneath. We go to these lengths out of fear that if we don't hide our inadequacies, if the people around us see us for who we really are, they will reject us.

The fear of rejection is what makes vulnerability so scary. We wouldn't be afraid of being vulnerable if it didn't bring with it the heightened possibility of being hurt, but that is what it means to be vulnerable. By definition, being vulnerable means we are open to being hurt, at risk of being taken advantage of, in danger of being rejected. And that sort of possibility is simply too terrifying for most of us, so we put on these masks to hide the parts of ourselves that we are ashamed of, buoyed by the belief that people will be more apt to accept us if they believe that our masks are our true selves.

In his famous poem *We Wear the Mask*, Poet Paul Laurence Dunbar captures the conflicting emotions that churn beneath the masks we wear. Though he acknowledges the deep seated anguish many of us feel, he lays bare the primal need to keep our pain hidden from the world behind our masks.

> *We wear the mask that grins and lies,*
> *It hides our cheeks and shades our eyes,—*
> *This debt we pay to human guile;*
> *With torn and bleeding hearts we smile,*
> *And mouth with myriad subtleties.*
>
> *Why should the world be over-wise,*
> *In counting all our tears and sighs?*
> *Nay, let them only see us, while*
>   *We wear the mask.*
>
> *We smile, but, O great Christ, our cries*
> *To thee from tortured souls arise.*
> *We sing, but oh the clay is vile*
> *Beneath our feet, and long the mile;*

> *But let the world dream otherwise,*
> *We wear the mask!*[14]

As Dunbar so eloquently expresses, we strap on our masks and present a false persona to the world, a carefully crafted disguise that reflects who we wish we were, not who we really are. We stifle our raw, unexamined emotions, hiding them beneath our forced smiles where they can eat away at our soul like termites underneath a fresh coat of paint. The problem with this defense mechanism, however, is that even if people do accept the version of ourselves that we show to them, they have accepted an impostor. They don't even know the real us, only the false persona we've presented to them. But it gets worse.

The vicious irony is that, in our attempts to avoid rejection from other people, we actually reject ourselves. We sit in judgement upon ourselves and conclude that we are not acceptable as we are, so we try to cover our imperfections and present a better, more sanitized version to the world. Then, since we have established our relationships under a false identity, we are forced to maintain our carefully crafted facades for the rest of the relationship or else face the possibility of rejection. In short, we go into hiding so that people can't reject the real us. Sadly, they also never get to *know* the real us.

In the original *Star Wars* trilogy, there is only one moment in which we get a glimpse of the human beneath the black mask. Anakin Skywalker (Darth Vader) has just destroyed the evil Emperor in order to save his son Luke Skywalker, though Vader is mortally wounded in the process. Luke tries to help him into an escape shuttle, but Anakin falls to the ground and asks for his son to help him remove the helmet so that he can look upon his boy with his own eyes. Sadly, Anakin had spent his son's entire life hidden behind that mask, separated by the dark veneer that elicited such fear and respect. It is only in the moment of his death that he is willing to let the pretenses drop and be vulnerable before his boy.

How many of us go through life hiding behind a similar set of masks, separated from the ones we love by a false persona that we constructed in order to protect ourselves?! My prayer is that you do not wait until it's too late to remove the masks that you hide behind.

Think About It –

- Take a look back over the list of masks described in this chapter. Which of them do you tend to put on? Are there any other masks that you'd add to this list?

- What do the masks you put on protect you from?

- What does it cost you to wear these masks?

CHAPTER 5

The Social Chameleon

I'll be anything you want. Just tell me what you want and I'll be that.
— Nicholas Sparks, *The Notebook*

Maggie has a problem. Although she has no trouble meeting wonderful guys and finding plenty of things they share in common, when it comes to commitment, she invariably gets cold feet. It's not that she hasn't tried to commit. In fact, she has been engaged four times and she has planned four weddings, but when it comes time to say "I do," she just can't. Regardless of how well suited each guy seems to be for her, despite how much they seem to have in common, as soon she dons that wedding dress, she is overwhelmed by the conviction that she is making a terrible mistake. So rather than walk down the aisle, she ends up running away. This is the premise of the romantic comedy *The Runaway Bride*.

On the surface, it may seem that Maggie Carpenter, played by Julia Roberts, has commitment issues. But as the movie progresses, it becomes evident that her problems are much deeper and that her fears of marrying for the wrong reasons are well founded. You see, Maggie is a social chameleon. She doesn't keep meeting great guys with whom she had a lot in common because she's lucky; rather, it's because she unconsciously changes her personality to match theirs. If they like sports, she likes sports. If they are into fishing, she is into fishing. The fact is she doesn't even realize she is doing it; but when it comes time to tie the knot, her subconscious mind screams *"Run!"* and she listens.

In the movie, Maggie begins to recognize her issue when someone asks her how she likes her eggs cooked. She automatically responds with how her last fiancé liked his eggs cooked. When pressed to describe how *she* likes them, she can't give an answer. She has become so used to shifting to match the people around her that she has lost touch with her own preferences. She has become the Social Chameleon.

Conforming to Our Surroundings

Can you identify with Maggie? I sure can. Looking back over the last couple of decades, particularly my twenties, I can clearly see the ways in which I would adjust myself to fit into whatever social grouping I was in at that time.

At my job, I was the stoic worker-bee, proving my worth through the quality and quantity of my labor. At church, I was the joyful worshipper who was always happy to jump in when something needed to get done. Around my friends, I was silly and sarcastic. Now, each of these qualities is a part of who I am, but I was intentionally overemphasizing different aspects of my personality to fit into whatever environment I was in at the time. I was creating warped caricatures of myself. In short, I was being a social chameleon.

In nature, a chameleon changes its color to blend into its surroundings. This ability is a crucial defense mechanism, because a predator cannot eat what it cannot see. In the same way, social chameleons change their personalities to fit into the social spheres that they inhabit. They become students of the people around them, watching how they speak, how they dress, how they interact, what they value. Then the social chameleon begins to adjust their own dress, attitude and behaviors accordingly. How drastically they alter themselves is dependent upon their desired result. Some social chameleons may simply try to blend into the crowd, while others will attempt to stand out from it. Regardless of their goal, the means to the end is the same: they become what they think other people expect them to be.

I did this without even thinking about it. At my job, I figured they wanted a hard worker who didn't complain. So that's who I became. I stifled my silly side and focused on doing my work as quickly and efficiently as possible (admittedly, precision was never my strong suit). When I'd finish one project, I would walk up to my boss, with a stoic face and my hands clasped behind my back like I was in military formation, and ask if there was something else I could do. Though I'd never bring it up, I was secretly hoping he would notice how quickly I had completed whatever task he'd given me and be impressed. Looking back, I can't help but shake my head at how ridiculously robotic I appeared. But in my young mind, I was just trying to prove that I was a mature and indispensable part of the team.

That same evening, I might hang out with friends and a completely different Eric would emerge. Gone would be the stoic, serious countenance that I wore at work, and in its place I would put on a grin and try to make people laugh by any means necessary. I would work through my humor arsenal, looking for the most effective tactic to entertain my audience: sarcasm, physical humor, bad puns, random comments that I found funny and insightful, but usually left other people confused and looking for the connection. I would even resort to self-deprecating humor, playing the lovable idiot, because I figured that making people laugh meant that they liked me, even if they were laughing at me.

As the social chameleon, the most important thing I could garner was the approval of my peers, my bosses, and the random person behind the counter at Starbucks. Because of my deep-seated insecurity, I looked to others around me for the validation I so desperately craved.

Validate Me

The cry of the social chameleon is for acceptance. We simply want to know that we are ok and that we are loved. The problem is that underneath the smiling face and confident exterior we don't feel ok; we don't feel all that lovable. So what do we do? We look to other people to give us the confidence that we are lacking. We ask them, "Am I enough?" Of course we don't trust that we are enough just as we are, so we become what we think they want us to be. It's as if we put a sign around our necks that says "Validate Me" and then begin to perform for other people's approval.

"You want me to look a certain way? I can do that." So we starve ourselves; we exercise obsessively; we lie about our age, cake on layers of makeup and even surgically alter our bodies so that we can garner the attention that we so frantically desire.

"You want me to act a certain way? No problem." So we alter our attitude, our vocabulary, our lifestyle, even our values. We willingly change ourselves in the hopes that we will be deemed acceptable.

It is truly amazing how much power we give broken people to influence our self-worth. We give people that we wouldn't trust to watch our goldfish the right to define us. And as author Leslie Vernick points out, "when you give another person the power to define you, then you also give them the power to control you."[15] So we willingly bend over backwards to conform to their expectations, hoping that if we become who we think they want us to be, they will give us their stamp of approval and we will finally feel valuable.

Of course this puts our identities in a precarious position. If we give people the right to tell us we are ok, then we are also giving them the ability to reject us. If we look to them to build us up, then we run the risk of being torn down by their disapproval. And our only protection against being crushed by the dissatisfaction of our parents, our peers and our coworkers is our performance.

We approach life like hamsters running on a wheel who

have become convinced that the only reason we are cared for and loved is because we run. So, since we've linked our value to our performance, we simply cannot stop running. Our deepest fear is that if we did rest, even for a moment, then our carefully crafted facades would come crashing down around us and we would be exposed as the charlatans that we really are. If we were to stop performing for the people around us, they might realize that we, like the Wizard of Oz, are not nearly as great and powerful as we have led them to believe. Our need to "always be on" is fueled by the subconscious belief that if people actually saw us for who we are, they would reject us. So we run, driven by our fear of rejection.

Of course, this means that we can never let our guard down around other people; we can never have a bad day, since we are only as good as our last performance. We wake up each morning with the need to prove our worth. Each interaction with a peer, each phone call, each pop quiz or work assignment is another test. Even our hobbies can become wrapped up in this need to earn our validation.

For instance, I love to play basketball. Get me on a basketball court with a few other people and I get as giddy as a school girl at a Taylor Swift concert. But throughout my twenties and early thirties, my play was haunted by the underlying need to prove my worth. I was always grinning at the beginning of a basketball game, but how I felt walking off the court at the end of the game would vary radically based upon how well I had played. It became a running joke in my house that my wife could tell how well the game went based upon how I would say "hi" when I got home. Apparently the tone of my voice betrayed how I felt about my performance.

Someone might say, "You were just being competitive. There's nothing wrong with that." I agree that there is nothing wrong with being competitive, so long as we don't forget that people are more important than winning and that our value isn't derived from whether we win or lose. After all, it's just a game. But in those days when I didn't feel secure in my identity, it was much more than a game. It was a way to prove my worth to both my teammates and myself. From the moment I stepped on the court, I was driven not only by my competitive nature, but also by my insecurity. The better I did, the more validation I got, which only solidified the veneer I'd built around my fear that there was nothing remarkable about me.

The sad truth is, when we set out to win other people's approval, everything we put our hands to is warped by the need to prove our worth through our performance. We will change our masks to fit each social situation we encounter throughout the day. And when we finally crash into bed at night, after a day filled with performing for other's approval, our thoughts will be plagued by second guessing: "I wish I hadn't said that. I must have looked like such an idiot. If only I could do it over again, I would..." Our minds will still be nitpicking our performance as we drift off to sleep, and when we wake up the next day, we will resign ourselves to proving our worth all over again. What an exhausting way to live!

The 20-40-60 Rule

It is probably not be as bad as you think.

Sure, you beat yourself up over the littlest mistake. You lay in bed at night second guessing what people thought when you did this or said that. But chances are the people around you are not nearly as critical of you as you are of yourself. Actress Shirley MacLaine is the outspoken champion of the 20-40-60 Rule, which goes something like this:

> *At 20, you are constantly worried about what others think about you.*
> *At 40, you stop caring as much about what others think about you.*
> *And at 60, you realize that nobody has been thinking about you nearly as much as you think they have.*[16]

Why? Because they have been far too busy thinking about themselves!

The people in your life are not lying in bed criticizing your every word and gesture. If they are thinking about an interaction you had with them, more than likely they are focused on their side of the conversation, not yours. It's similar to the way we assess whether a photograph is good or bad. We tend to look at ourselves first, and only afterwards see the other people in the picture. If our eyes are closed or we look odd in any way, then regardless of how everyone else in the picture looks, we deem it a bad photo. Conversely, if we like how we look, then chances are we will deem it good, even if the other people in the picture look horrible. In the same way, we are far more critical of ourselves than we are of anyone else. We are also far more aware of our mistakes and our underlying insecurities than anyone else is.

So don't waste too much time worrying about what other people are thinking about you, because chances are they're not thinking about you at all.

Gaining Approval but Losing Ourselves

> *Two roads diverged in a wood, and I—*
> *I took the one less traveled by,*
> *And that has made all the difference.*
> - from *The Road Not Taken* by Robert Frost[17]

As we already saw in the last chapter, the danger of hiding behind a mask and performing is that we present a false-self to the world. We pretend to be someone that we are not, so even if our greatest desire is realized and we succeed in winning our peers' approval, they are not actually accepting us. Rather, they are accepting the persona that we've fabricated; they are approving of the masks that we wear, rather than the real, flesh and blood person beneath the mask.

Unfortunately, the real us is just as lonely and isolated as ever, buried under a disguise. Sure, it cries out to be loved and accepted, but we distract ourselves from its cries and dull the pain. And if we keep at it long enough, if we bury it deeply enough and stifle its cries with enough pain killers, then eventually we might even convince ourselves that we are who we pretend to be.

That's the problem with becoming a social chameleon: if you do it long enough, eventually you lose sight of who you are. You begin to believe that you are the masks you wear. After all, if you can't lie to yourself, who can you lie to? As Nathaniel Hawthorne pointed out in his novel *The Scarlet Letter*, "No man, for any considerable period, can wear one face to himself and another to the multitude, without finally getting bewildered as to which may be the true."[18]

So we go through life thinking that we are being authentic, yet all the while we are rotating through a handful of masks, shifting and morphing to fit in. Then one day our masks slip and we hear a cry from deep inside. Or perhaps someone asks us how we like our eggs, and we can't give them an answer. At that point, we have a choice: we can either run to our bag of masks and slip on a few more or, like a child who sees the corner of the wallpaper sticking up, we can begin peeling our masks away to see what lies underneath. I don't need to tell you which one is the scarier option.

We have been covering our nakedness and vulnerability for so long that it has become second nature. Sadly, it has also left us in the state we're in, hidden in plain sight behind a bunch of masks and false pretenses. Thankfully, there is another option available to us, one which few people choose: we can choose to pull away the masks, choose to stop numbing ourselves to the internal cry for love and acceptance and see what is really underneath it all. It's a terrifying thought, to be exposed and naked, even to ourselves, but it's also the only way we will ever find authentic love and genuine acceptance.

It is the path less traveled, but if we should choose to take it, then it will make all the difference in the world.

Coming Clean

If you went into the doctor's office with a large bandage over a cut, what's the first thing the doctor would do? She would remove it in order to see what's going on under there, right? And if there is an infection, the sunlight and fresh air will actually help the healing process while keeping the wound covered will only make it worse. Revealing is the first step toward healing.

I can vividly remember one of the first times I was willing to strip off my masks and be fully vulnerable with my wife, Cathy. We were returning home from a weekend away to celebrate our fifth wedding anniversary. During that long car ride home, we began discussing the state of our marriage, and it wasn't all positive. As the conversation grew in intensity, I started to feel pretty defensive. So I resorted to my mask of choice when I feel attacked: I got angry in the hopes that she would either see my perspective or just leave me alone.

Of course it didn't work out the way I'd hoped. Rather than making the car ride more comfortable, it only heightened the intensity. Eventually our conversation got so ugly and I got so defensive that I snapped and did the most reasonable thing I could think of in that moment: I pulled over and told her to drive home. I, in my need to avoid the tension, would find another way to get home. Admittedly, my plan wasn't very well thought out. I didn't even know what county we were in. However, my ploy did succeed in getting her to go silent, which certainly wasn't good for our relationship, but at least it gave me a momentary break from conflict.

When we finally got home, however, we could no longer avoid the elephant in the room. I wanted to hold onto my anger. I felt it was justified. Yet, during the silence of the ride I had also become aware of something deeper, stirring underneath the anger, crying to be noticed. As I sat with it, I began to realize that this was the nerve that had been struck, this was the reason I'd instinctively put on my mask of anger. It was a feeling of inadequacy, a feeling that was dripping in shame. Without even thinking about it, I had tried to bury it. But as I sat there on the couch, I realized that hiding this feeling would only push us further apart. So in a moment of reckless abandon, I moved my masks to the side and gave voice to the cry inside.

I said: "Cathy, I feel like a failure as a husband. We've been married five years and I still don't have a clue how to love you or to communicate with you in the way you want. And I'm scared that I'll never figure out how to do it."

As I confessed, my anger retreated and tears began to flow. It was one of the first times in our relationship that I was allowing Cathy into an area of shame and vulnerability while I was still struggling with it. Admittedly, it was terrifying to pull away the mask of anger and let her in. I was showing her the real me, the weak me who didn't have it all together, and I was making myself vulnerable to rejection.

I'll never forget her response. Before I opened up, she had been at the far end of the couch, with crossed arms and hardened heart, but as I brought my defenses down and pulled aside my mask, she softened as well. Before I knew it, she was at my side, with her arms around me. And later that evening, she confessed that she had never felt closer to me than when I had opened up and allowed myself to be vulnerable.

Talk about irony! From my perspective, dragging that dark pearl of shame into the light had been an embarrassing admission of weakness. I was terrified to admit it, because it might cause her to think less of me. But it elicited exactly the opposite response from my wife. Rather than rejecting me, she actually moved toward me, since we were no longer separated by the masks I'd been hiding behind. What a liberating feeling, to know that I didn't need to perform for my wife's approval. What a beautiful realization that I could come just as I was and be loved just as I am.

God has designed us to live before Him and one another in complete intimacy, naked and unashamed, and for one shining moment I was able to drop the pretense and rest in the magnificence of His design. Sadly, a moment of intimate transparency cannot overcome a lifetime of hiding in the shadows, and eventually I reaffixed the mask over my nakedness and went back to proving my worth.

The fact is circumstances may force us to drop our masks and step into the light from time to time, but we will never be able to scrape together enough courage to actually stay in the light on our own. So long as we perceive our true selves as unacceptable, we will be tempted to hide them. Until we can rest in the belief that we are loved, we will attempt to perform for the approval of our peers. Before we can hope to rest in the light, a fundamental shift must take place in our self-perception. Otherwise, we will continue running back into the shadows and hiding behind our masks.

Think About It –

- Would you consider yourself to be a social chameleon? In what ways are you altering yourself to fit your environment?

- Eric equated performing for other's approval to a hamster ceaselessly running on its wheel. Does this approach to life sound familiar? Are you living each day with the need to prove your worth?

- Whose opinions are you most concerned about and in what ways have you conformed to their expectations so that they will validate you?

PART TWO
Image Restoration

Now, with God's help, I shall become myself.
— Søren Kierkegaard

CHAPTER 6

Diamonds in the Rough

Thou hast made man for thyself,
and he is restless until he rests in Thee.
- Augustine

When it comes to television, I've got a guilty pleasure, but it has nothing to do with sports, zombies, crime scene investigation or super heroes. My guilty pleasure is watching shows about antiques. Admittedly, my wife doesn't understand my fascination. She laughs that I will flip past singing competitions and sporting events, but then stop as soon as I see someone searching through an old garage or storage unit. Shows like that tap into a part of my heart that never quite grew up, a part of me that still dreams of finding buried treasure. Only in these shows, the treasures are buried in forgotten storage units and attics, covered in dust and memories.

There are a lot of shows about antiquing now, but the original program that first got me hooked is called *Antiques Roadshow*. In each episode, ordinary people bring their family heirlooms that have been gathering dust in the attic or in a closet somewhere and experts tell them what they are worth. Many of the items that people bring are relatively worthless, but every once in a while someone will carry in something in that is truly rare, something far more valuable than anyone could have guessed.

I enjoy trying to guess what is and isn't valuable, but I've found that I'm pretty awful at it. My problem is that I judge things by their appearance. If something looks well cared for, I tend to think it's more valuable than another, similar item that is beat up and weathered. But here's the thing with antiques: an item's condition isn't nearly as important as who made it. For instance, one guy brought in an ornate sewing table that I would have been proud to have in my home. It was beautiful, with long, fluted legs and intricate, hand-carved details. Plus, it was in cherry condition; however, the expert didn't dwell on the table's condition. Rather, he turned it over and began to point out all of the little, easily overlooked details that proved this particular table was a reproduction. It turns out that it had simply been made to look old, and the man who had brought it in was disappointed when he discovered it wasn't worth much.[19]

In contrast, a woman brought in an old, rickety card table that she'd purchased at a garage sale for $25. The thing looked like it had been thrown down several flights of steps. There were chips and dings everywhere. I would have been tempted to use it for firewood. Once again, however, the furniture expert looked beyond its condition to the maker's mark on the underside of the table top. It had been hand-made sometime during the 1790's by John Seymour and Son in Boston. The maker's stamp was barely visible through all the grime, but it was there. Then the appraiser shocked this unsuspecting woman, suggesting that it was easily worth $200,000, perhaps going as high as $300,000 on a good day at auction.[20] She was understandably floored, but this story doesn't stop there. A year later, she sold the card table at auction for $490,000, a price that was nearly 20,000 times what she'd paid for it![21] Now do you see why I love watching this sort of show so much?!

My point is that something's value is not always dependent upon its outward beauty, its functionality or even its condition. Often the most important thing is who made it. This same principle applies to us.

Beat Up Masterpieces

In chapter two, we saw that God created us in His image, so we are of unimaginable worth. However, due to the effects of the Fall, our self-image has been warped by sin and tarnished by shame and guilt. When we look at ourselves (or other people for that matter) we don't see what God sees. Rather, we see the ravages of sin. We see the ways that we don't measure up to other people's expectations, whether spoken or unspoken. We can't help but compare ourselves to the airbrushed images gracing the magazine covers in the checkout aisle and the comparison isn't encouraging. When we look at them, we see the flawless smile, the confident exterior. Then we look at ourselves and we notice all the dings and scratches, many of them self-inflicted. So we don't feel valuable. To be honest, we don't even feel acceptable. We feel down right embarrassed about what we see and we go out of our way to hide the evidence.

Of course this begs the question: What does God see when He looks at us? We are going to explore this question in greater detail through the next several chapters, but I will give one brief answer here: He sees a priceless work of art that He created.

Is that hard for you to accept? Perhaps you're thinking, "You don't know me, so how could you possibly say I'm a priceless work of art?"

I don't need to know you in order to say it with confidence, because God's Word already proclaims it. Ephesians 2:10 declares that "we are God's masterpiece. He has created us anew in Christ Jesus, so we can do the good things he planned for us long ago" (Ephesians 2:10 NLT). Did you get that? The one who spoke the universe into existence and is responsible for every glorious sunrise and sunset calls YOU His masterpiece!

You might be thinking, "Oh, that's just a word some translator picked out. The Bible wasn't written in English after all."

Fair enough. The original word that Paul used to describe us is *poema,* from which we get the word "poem." In other words, you are God's poem, His work of art that bears His fingerprints and reveals His heart. As someone who has dabbled in poetry, I can attest to the fact that each poem I write is a unique reflection of a part of me; each one is an attempt to externalize some thought or feeling with words. And I have a paternal fondness for each of my poems, like a parent has for his newborn baby. I am simultaneously proud and protective of them, sharing them with others as if I were entrusting them with a precious part of myself. When someone finishes reading one and I see that it has elicited the intended emotional response, I can't help but feel joy. Conversely, if someone approaches one of my works with an over-critical attitude, focusing only on the flaws, I tend to get a little defensive for this expression of my heart.

I suspect that God feels that way about us. Of course, His sense of self-worth isn't affected by whether or not we appreciate each person for the unique work of art that they are. However, in the same way that I am intimately attached to my works of artistic expression, He is intimately attached to us. Each and every one of us uniquely bears His image, so when someone dismisses or demeans one of His masterpieces, it naturally grieves Him. So imagine how He must feel when His masterpieces begin to dismiss or demean themselves!

Consider how often and how easily we sit in judgement upon ourselves. We curse the body that God has given us, calling it names like ugly, disgusting, pathetic. We don't like the way that God made us, so we go out of our way to become someone else. We even downplay the gifts He's entrusted to our care and tell ourselves that we couldn't possibly be used by Him. Far too many of us act as our own harshest critics and then point at our Creator and declare, "I am a mistake!"

However, Ephesians 2:10 reminds us that we are anything but mistakes! We are His masterpieces, remade in Christ so that we can do the work He has uniquely planned for each of us. This verse reminds us that in our Father's eyes we have both value and purpose. Sadly, most of us struggle to see ourselves through our Father's eyes. Rather, we tend to view ourselves through sin-tainted glasses, which hinder us from recognizing the priceless works of art that we are. All we can see are the dings and scratches, so we deem ourselves worthless, damaged and unusable. This warped self-perception not only demeans God's masterpieces; all too often it also causes us to disqualify ourselves from doing the very work He created us to do in the first place.

Far too many of us go through life believing lies about ourselves that grieve the heart of our Creator. We could look to Him for our approval, but instead we tend to look to other broken, insecure creatures and allow them to determine our worth.

When We Worship Man's Opinion More Than God's

"Worship" is a word that's so familiar to us that we've lost sight of its true meaning. We tend to think that it simply refers to the songs that we sing during a church service, but worship is so much more than that! Worship literally means "to ascribe worth" to something. When we worship something, we deem it to be of such great value that we are willing to order our lives around it. We are willing to sacrifice other valuable things in order to make it a central component of our lives.

For example, if we worship a band, we will gladly sacrifice time and money to see them in concert. We will part with our hard-earned cash to buy tickets, then drive for hours to the venue, only to sing along to songs that we have heard countless times. And we will do so joyfully. Similarly, if we worship physical fitness, we will order our lives around staying in shape. We will limit the amount of food we eat and sacrifice sleep in order to get to the gym. These are just a couple of the myriad things we tend to worship.

The Bible declares that God alone is worthy of our worship, but that doesn't mean that we worship Him alone. In fact, when we begin to feel insecure, our natural impulse is to run to anyone who can validate us. And in order to earn that validation, we willingly order our lives around their expectations. We become who we think they want us to be in order to earn what we fear we cannot do without: their approval. In fact, many of us get more fixated on what other people think about us than what God thinks about us. When this happens, we give others, rather than God, the right to influence our thoughts, choices and actions. In a way, we put them on the throne of our hearts, a throne that rightfully belongs to our Creator. This impulse to value others' opinions over and above God's is nothing new. Sadly, it's all too common to man in the aftermath of the Fall.

Perhaps the most powerful example of how other people's opinions can eclipse that of our Creator is found in the twelfth chapter of John's Gospel. As we pick up the story, Jesus is near the end of his public ministry and he is making quite a stir in Jerusalem. Not only has he been feeding multitudes and driving out demons, but he has just raised a guy named Lazarus from the dead! Between his authoritative teaching and his outstanding miracles, people are beginning to openly wonder, "Could he be the long awaited Messiah?" The Pharisees, the Jewish religious experts, are quick to deny this suggestion, in spite of all they have seen and heard.

Admittedly, there are many of the Jewish leaders who do believe that Jesus is God's anointed Messiah. However, they are unwilling to voice their belief "for fear that they would be put out of the synagogue; *for they loved the approval of men rather than the approval of God*" (John 12:42-43 NASB, emphasis added).

What a tragic statement. They recognize Jesus for who he is, but they are unwilling to voice their beliefs out of fear of being publically ostracized. They place a greater value on the opinions of their peers than that of their Creator.

Now, we may shake our heads at those insecure leaders who would compromise their convictions because of social pressure, but I suspect that we are just as guilty as they were. Despite how often in scripture God claims to love us, most of us don't believe Him. We don't feel worthy of His love. We still feel overwhelmingly deficient and so, like Adam and Eve with the fruit, we take matters into our own hands. We seek to make ourselves worthy through our own efforts.

Earning our Identity (DO → BE)

The couple sat in my office, their seats separated from one another by inches but their hearts by miles. They were going through one of those rough patches that many recently-married couples hit, when the quirks they'd considered cute while dating start to become irritating in marriage. I hadn't been married much longer than these two, but I sat there nodding as if I had seen this problem a hundred times. On the surface I may have seemed cool, calm and collected, but inside I was full of anxious energy.

This was my first pastoral counseling session with a couple and I didn't want to mess it up. As I sat there, listening to them process their frustrations, I felt an overwhelming need to find the solution to their problems. I wanted to say something that would cause them to suddenly realize how much they loved one another, so that they would walk out of my office arm in arm, rather than up in arms. Now, I'd like to say that my sole motivation was my desire to see them have a happier, healthier marriage, but in reality I needed them to go away pleased with my counseling so that it would affirm that I was in the right field. In a twisted sort of way, I (the pastor) was asking the people I was counseling to tell me I was ok! I was asking them to minister to me, when it should have been the other way around.

Welcome to the warped existence of the performer. When we are not secure in our identity, we feel the pressure to prove our worth in everything that we do. We DO something in order to BE something. I wanted to be a good pastor, but I didn't feel secure in that role. So I tried really hard to prove that I was worthy to be called a pastor, both to the couple in my office as well as to myself. I was DOing in order to BE. Sound familiar?

This is a remarkably common approach to life that most of us operate from without even realizing it. We decide in our mind that we want to be something, but since we don't feel worthy of that designation yet, we set out to make ourselves worthy through our effort. The problem with this approach to life is that our self-image becomes completely dependent upon our performance. So long as we perform well, we feel worthy. But the moment we mess up or have a bad showing, our self-esteem tanks. Unfortunately, when our identity is tied to our performance, we are only as good as our last effort. This means that we can never rest, never take a day off and never let our guard down. It's an exhausting way to live. But what's the alternative?

Resting in our Identity (BE → DO)

In contrast to my anxious attempts to prove my worthiness as a pastor, consider the way Jesus approached his ministry: he never went out of his way to meet people's expectations or told them what they wanted to hear just to make them happy. When he encountered opposition, as he did regularly from the Jewish religious leaders, he didn't alter his approach to appease the naysayers. He simply went about the work that the Father had given him to do. What was the secret to his confidence? At his core, Jesus knew who he was and he knew what he was about - He was God's son and he was about his Father's business. Therefore, he never worried about the opinions of the crowds or went out of his way to earn their approval. He never put on a mask or performed for validation. He simply rested in his identity and ministered out of it.[22]

Imagine if you were that confident in your identity! Think about how different your approach to life would be if you could fully rest in the person that God has created you to be. You would no longer need to look to other people for your validation, because you would already know deep down that you were beautifully and wonderfully made. Since you already knew of your incalculable worth, you wouldn't need to try and prove your worth through everything you did. Instead, you could embrace your roles and responsibilities with joy and intentionality, not anxiety. After all, even if you fell flat on your face, it wouldn't affect your identity one iota. You'd be free to be the person God made you to be and the world would be a much richer place because of it.

So how do we get there? How can we begin to embrace our true, God-given identity, rather than buying into sin's warped suggestion that our value is dependent upon how we look and how useful we make ourselves? I can tell you it won't come from simply trying harder. That's the knee-jerk impulse of the performer. Instead, like the prodigal child who has run far from home and wound up covered in the muck of the pigsty, we must turn our hearts back toward our Father and allow Him to clean us up and restore our perception of ourselves.

If we hope to find our true identity, then we must come to the One who gave it to us in the first place. You and I each bear the maker's mark of our Father in Heaven. He made us and His opinion about us is the only one that truly matters. So let's spend some time exploring what He has to say about us.

Think About It –

- Ephesians 2:10 declares that "we are God's masterpiece." Do you have a hard time accepting that you are a priceless work of the Master's hands? Why or why not?

- Despite God's insistence that we are His masterpiece, the world around us can be a lot less encouraging, and it's easy to allow these critical words to shape our self-image. What sort of critical words have been spoken over you? How have they shaped the way you see yourself?

- Often, we are our own harshest critics, focusing on our flaws rather than appreciating God's workmanship. In what ways has self-criticism colored the way you view yourself and influenced the way you live?

- In this chapter, we discussed two different approaches to life: Some of us are driven by insecurity, so we do things in order to become the person we want to be. Others of us are able to rest in our God-given identity, and everything we do flows out of the security we find in Him. Which of these best describes your current approach to life: **DO → BE** or **BE → DO**?

- How has this approach influenced the choices you've made in life?

- How has it influenced the way you relate to God and others?

CHAPTER 7

A New Creation

There is no saint without a past, no sinner without a future.
– Augustine of Hippo

A few years back, my wife and I ran across some old family photos as we were cleaning out her mother's attic. They were black and white and the passage of time had taken its toll on them. One picture in particular captured my wife's attention. It was an old family photo taken in front of her grandparents' farmhouse. Cathy's mother, who was just a toddler at the time, was playing on the lawn while Cathy's grandparents stoically looked on from the porch.

Unfortunately, this particular picture was badly damaged. Not only had the image faded over time, but rough handling had worn away the edges so that entire portions of the photo were missing. Had it not been such a valuable treasure, we might have been tempted to throw it away, but it was irreplaceable and priceless. We couldn't fix it by ourselves, but thankfully there was someone we could take it to who had the ability to undo the ravages of time.

We dropped the picture off at a photo restoration specialist and when we picked it up a few days later, the changes were miraculous. What had been a damaged and faded picture was now vibrant and complete. The sharpness of the image had been increased as if someone had stripped away layers of grime and the missing portions had somehow been recreated. It was a brand new picture and we proudly framed it and hung it in our home for all to see.

Tarnished Images

You and I are a lot like that old photo.

We have been made in God's image and, therefore, have an innate value, but over time the image has been smudged and smeared to the point that it's nearly unrecognizable. We have opened our heart to others and had it broken as a result. We have tried to accomplish great things and failed miserably. We have declared our desire to die to our flesh and live for Christ, but our flesh is a whole lot more resilient than we had anticipated. So we don't feel like image-bearers; we feel more like failures.

In all honesty, we are failures. Sorry if that sounds harsh, but it's the truth. We have failed to faithfully represent God's heart to mankind. We have failed to care for His creation. We have failed to love our neighbor as ourselves. We have failed to be holy as He is holy. The fact is we are flawed, distorted image-bearers. We are sinners.

Sin is an archery term that describes any shot that misses the bulls-eye. In the Bible, sin refers to any thought, statement or deed that is less than God's perfect, righteous standard. Truth be told, none of us have lived up to that standard. Every single one of us has sinned; every one of us has missed the mark. As Paul points out, "there is no one righteous, not even one" (Romans 3:10). John makes the same point, stating in no uncertain terms that "if we claim to be without sin, we deceive ourselves" (1 John 1:8).

You and I have sinned and the Bible is clear as to the consequence of our sin: "the wages of sin is death" (Romans 6:23). God warned Adam and Eve in the Garden that if they ate of the forbidden fruit, they would die. Of course, their disobedience didn't lead to their immediate demise, but death still entered creation. God cursed mankind's bodies so that they would break down and ultimately die. "From dust you have been made and to dust you shall return"

(Genesis 3:19). So physical death is a consequence of sin; however, there is a second painful ramification of our sin - it separates us from relationship with our Creator. This separation is what theologians refer to as "spiritual death."

At one point in Israel's history, the chosen people of God began to wonder aloud why their God had gone silent and wouldn't respond to their prayers. The prophet Isaiah responded, "It's your sins that have cut you off from God. Because of your sins, He has turned away and will not listen anymore" (Isaiah 59:2 NLT). You see, our God is a holy God. He is not plagued by things like selfishness, lust, pettiness, addiction or insecurity. That's what "holy" means: "other than the ordinary." His perfection stands in sharp contrast to the brokenness we see in the world around us. He is holy, and He calls mankind to be holy like He is holy.[23] Unfortunately, although we were fashioned in His image, sin has crept in like a virus and twisted His good and perfect design. Though we are called to reflect His holy nature, we find ourselves completely unable to do so. And our Creator will not stomach our sin. It is like a horrid stench in his nostrils.

Our sin not only causes our Creator to turn away from us, it causes us to run from Him. Shortly after their disobedience, when Adam and Eve heard the Lord's voice, they hid from Him. Sin drove them into hiding and it does the same to us. Our sin drives a wedge between us and our Creator. Why? Because our sin is fundamentally incompatible with God's holiness. They cannot coexist in the same space any more than darkness can coexist in the same space as light.

Don't get me wrong. It's not that God cannot survive in the presence of sinfulness. Rather, sin cannot survive in the presence of His holiness. Just as darkness is destroyed by the presence of light, mankind would be utterly destroyed if we were to come face to face with our holy, righteous Creator in the midst of our sin. So like two magnets whose poles are reversed, our sin hinders us from drawing close to our God; it pushes us away from the intimate relationship that He desires to have with us.

Welcome to the human predicament: we have been designed to remain intimately connected with our God as we represent Him in His creation, but our sin severs that connection and hinders our ability to faithfully represent Him. However, that desire for connection with our Creator doesn't go away simply because we are estranged from Him. We cannot shut off the feeling that we were made for so much more than this broken existence within which we find ourselves. Furthermore, as we saw in chapter three, God frustrated the very things we would normally be drawn toward in order to find fulfillment and purpose. He cursed Eve's role as both mother and wife and He cursed the work of Adam's hands. In short, our Creator carved out a God-shaped hole in our most ancient ancestors that only He could fill. And since these curses still affect each of us today, that hole exists in each of us as well. Therefore, in spite of our sin, God has designed us to hunger for connection with Him.

Climbing Broken Stairways to Heaven

So here is the dilemma: we hunger for connection with our God, and yet we also have this sin that has left a chasm between Him and us. What can we do? Well, whenever we are faced with a problem, mankind has an innate tendency to try and deal with it on our own. We saw this tendency in Adam and Eve. When faced with their sin, they resorted to covering it up and hiding in the shadows. We are a lot like them, whether we recognize that fact or not. Our natural impulse is to try and fix our brokenness by our own strength.

One way that some of us deal with our dilemma is by silencing the cry of our hearts for intimate connection with God. Rather than trying to overcome our sinful nature, we resort to simply numbing out the cries of our conscience. We turn to painkillers like drugs, alcohol, pornography, shopping, or food in an effort to distract ourselves from the reality of our brokenness. Numbing out is one way to deal with our separation anxiety.

But sometimes we are not willing to turn a blind eye to our depravity. We are not willing to give up on our desire for connection with our God. So rather than drown out the cry for connection, we resort to figuring out some way to bridge the chasm that our sin has created between Him and us. We know that we haven't lived up to God's righteous standard and we set out to make up for our errors. We reason that if doing bad things got us into this predicament, then doing good things must be the way to dig ourselves out.

When we try and live up to God's standard by our own strength, rules take on a whole new purpose: they become like rungs on a ladder that we climb in an attempt to attain righteousness. Each rung of our ladder is composed of a different rule:

> Don't give into my addictive desires.
> Don't give into my anger.
> Don't give in to my sexual temptations.
> Don't root for the Yankees or the Raiders
> (that's a big one).
> Read at least two chapters of scripture every day.
> Pray at every meal.
> Fast at least once a month.

The list of "rules" we create is endless, especially since we tend to collect new ones from any number of sources: from the Bible, from our parents, from our pastor's sermons, from our peers. We build bigger and bigger ladders with more and more rungs. And we judge how we are doing by looking around us and seeing how we stack up to our neighbors, as if they are the standard by which God will judge us. Sure, sometimes we slip on a rung and fall down a bit, but so long as we are always moving up, so long as our good deeds outweigh our bad ones, and so long as we're doing better than the majority of people around us, then we figure God has got to accept us. After all, we're good people, right?

Sadly, no. Being a good person isn't enough. Doing more good deeds than bad ones isn't enough. And God doesn't grade on a curve. Our neighbors are not the standard by which we are judged; God is the standard. Which doesn't bode well for us, since God's standard is perfection. So, while any one of these rungs may be a wise approach to life, our perspective on them is fatally flawed when we begin to look to them as the means by which we can overcome our sins and earn God's approval.

No religious ladder can ever help us attain right standing in the eyes of the law. No amount of rule following can ever help us attain intimacy with God. In fact, it tends to do just the opposite. When we begin to focus on the rungs, on climbing the ladder, on beating our flesh into submission, we naturally take our eyes off of God and focus upon ourselves and our own determination.

Climbing Nowhere

Admittedly, one of the biggest temptations of any committed follower of Christ when faced with our imperfection is to try and make ourselves holy through our own efforts. In the Bible, it is called legalism; today we might call it moralism, but they are basically the same thing. We turn the biblical standards into a bunch of rules. Then we try to keep these rules by sheer grit and determination in order to earn God's favor.

This is what Jesus railed on the Pharisees for doing. The Pharisees were Jewish religious leaders who were so zealous about keeping God's laws that they not only observed the 613 commandments and regulations that they found in the Torah,[24] but added another 1,500 man-made rules that they used to protect God's commandments. In the same way that a parent erects a fence around a pool in order to keep the little ones from falling in, the Pharisees sought to put up so many obstacles that the people of Israel would never even get close to breaking one of God's laws.[25] Good desire; flawed approach.

Despite the Pharisees' dogged attempts to live righteously,

Jesus railed against their legalistic fixation on the law. He lamented that "these people honor me with their lips, but their hearts are far from me. They worship me in vain; their teachings are merely human rules" (Mark 7:6-7). Why was he so hard on them? One reason is that they got fixated on the rules, on the laws and traditions, but they completely disregarded God's heart. You can avoid murdering someone, but still harbor bitterness and anger in your heart. You can give 10% or even 20% of your income away and still be consumed by greed. You can abstain from sex outside of your marriage covenant and still be consumed by lust. You can go to church every weekend, read ten chapters of scripture every day, say a prayer at every meal, and still have little to no relationship with Jesus. Rules simply cannot make us more righteous; they just make us more religious and more self-reliant.

The second reason Jesus railed on the legalism of the Pharisees is that it turned the law into something that it was never intended to be – a way to save ourselves. By constructing ladders made of religious activities and thou-shalt-not's, the Pharisees convinced themselves that their righteousness was something that they could attain simply by obeying the rules. The problem is God never intended for mankind to attain righteousness through observing the Law. Paul made this point abundantly clear in his letter to the Galatians. He explained that "if a law had been given that could impart life, then righteousness would certainly have come by the law" (Galatians 3:21). But, as Paul explains, that was never the purpose of the law. Instead, it was designed to reveal our natural sinfulness and our desperate need for a savior. "So the law was put in charge to lead us to Christ that we might be justified by faith" (Galatians 3:24).

In other words, the law was never meant to be a religious ladder to climb. It was never intended to be the means by which we earn intimacy with God; rather, it was intended to reveal our utter brokenness so that we would come to the place where we willingly cry out for a savior to rescue us. In a lot of ways, the law is like getting an X-ray at the dentist's office. The X-ray doesn't heal our cavities, it simply reveals them and shows us how badly we need to see the dentist. In the same way, the law shines a spotlight on our depravity and drives us into the arms of our savior.

Someone might say, "What's the point of focusing on my depravity? Why would God go to all that effort just to show me how much I've fallen short? Why not just tell me I'm forgiven?" But the message of grace without a realization of our need for it is like a dentist offering to drill and fill our cavities for free when we don't even realize that we have them. No one would be excited for that offer, regardless of how generous it is. As the old hymn declares, "Amazing grace, how sweet the sound, that saved a wretch like me."[26] Grace sounds a whole lot sweeter when we recognize just how wretched we really are.

Good News

I've got some good news. God doesn't expect us to overcome the chasm that sin has created between us and Him. He is well aware of our inability to live up to His righteous standard on our own strength. So we can drop the ladders we have been constructing and stop trying to earn our righteousness, because our Creator has made a way for us sinners to be made right with Him. God has bridged the gap for us. Although we deserve death, He chose to give us new life. How? By taking the punishment we had earned and placing it upon Himself. This is the Good News, also known as the Gospel, which is declared throughout the pages of God's word. Here are just a few ways the Good News is articulated throughout scripture:

> Surely he took up our pain and bore our suffering,
> yet we considered him punished by God, stricken
> by him and afflicted. He was pierced for our
> transgressions, he was crushed for our iniquities;

the punishment that brought us peace was upon
him, and by his wounds we are healed. (Isaiah
53:4-5)[27]

For God so loved the world that he gave his one and
only Son, that whoever believes in him should not
perish but have eternal life. (John 3:16)

Christ carried the burden of our sins. He was nailed
to the cross, so that we would stop sinning and
start living right. By his cuts and bruises you are
healed. (1 Peter 2:24 CEV)

I could add so many more declarations of the gospel to this list:
Acts 13:38-39; Romans 3:21-26; Romans 4:25; 1 Corinthians 15:1-11;
2 Timothy 2:8; Titus 2:14; Hebrews 9:28; 1 Peter 3:18; 1 John 4:10.
There are even more than these in the pages of the Bible, but you
get the idea. All of these articulations of the Good News make the
same central point: Jesus died in our place, so that we could be freed
from our bondage to sin. He paid the penalty of our rebelliousness.
Because of Jesus's willingness to die for our sins, we no longer need
to accept death and eternal separation from God as our fate.

So despite the fact that we can't save ourselves, God has made a
way for us to be saved all the same. And the Old Testament Law and
the Prophets foretold that He would do this. It's not as if He intended
for mankind to live righteously by the law, and only decided to send
Jesus when it became apparent that we couldn't. This is no plan B.
This is, and always has been, God's primary plan to save mankind.
The law was given to show humanity our desperate need for a
savior, but God always knew He would ultimately need to make
us right in the eyes of the law - what we call being made righteous.
Through Jesus's death, we are given new life.

However, Christ's sacrifice did more than just pull us out of the
cosmic trashcan. Much like the photo restoration specialist did for

my old family picture, Jesus has literally restored us through his sacrifice. Paul put it this way: "If anyone is in Christ, he is a new creation, the old has gone and the new is come" (2 Corinthians 5:17). In other words, we are no longer defined by our sin. That's not to say that we cease to sin or to feel tempted by the things of this world. Addicts may still hear the siren-call of their drug of choice. Liars may still feel the urge to bend the truth. Whatever we struggled with prior to our conversion will probably still have a grip on our heart after our conversion. So what does it mean to be a New Creation?

What Paul is describing here is primarily a change to our legal standing, not our sin nature. We are like criminals who have been brought before a judge who just happens to also be our Father. Since He is righteous and just, He cannot simply turn a blind eye to our crimes. So He looks at the long list of our offenses and declares us to be guilty as charged. Furthermore, He imposes the appropriate penalty for our crimes - death.

But here's the thing: our God is not merely a righteous Judge. He is also a loving, merciful Father. Therefore, once He finishes reading the verdict, He takes off His judge's robes and walks down to stand beside us. Then He does something completely unexpected: He takes upon Himself the penalty that we have earned. He dies in our place, His life for ours. So when we walk out of the courtroom that day, it is not as death-row inmates condemned to die. Rather, it is as free men and women whose debts have been paid in full. Theologians call this "justification," since we have been justified in the eyes of the law - the old is gone and the new has come.

This means that we no longer need to remain estranged from our Father in Heaven, since we are no longer incompatible with Him. Our sins have been dealt with, covered by the blood of Christ. So we can stop hiding from our Creator and come before Him just as we are.

We prodigals can come home.

Accepting a Gift

You might be wondering, "What about my inclination to sin? If our God calls us to be holy as He is holy, then how can I do that when my flesh simply refuses to die? We will cover these questions in the next chapter. For now, however, there is another issue we need to deal with - our desire to earn God's grace.

You see, despite the fact that God has already bridged the chasm of sin for us, even though Jesus has already died for our sins, the little moralist inside each of us has a hard time accepting this. We like to view ourselves as self-made men and women. We don't want to be indebted to anyone. So if God wants to save us from our sins, great, but we are going to make sure we deserve it. Maybe it's a product of our upbringing. Perhaps it's too many Christmas warnings that if we aren't good, Santa will bring us coal instead of a new bike. For whatever reason, our natural inclination is to balk at the idea that God would simply forgive us out of love. We cannot fathom this sort of undeserved kindness, which the Bible refers to as grace. So instead of gratefully embracing God's gift of grace, we go out of our way to earn it.

Back when I was 12, I had a birthday party and invited a new boy from school to come. I barely knew him, but when it came time to open the presents it was his gift that blew all the others I got that day out of the water. It was a brand new video game for the original Nintendo Entertainment System. I don't remember which game it was anymore, but I do remember the embarrassment I felt for the extravagance of his gift. It was too much. I didn't deserve this. I'd only invited him on a whim. Looking back, it's ironic that I was conscience stricken over a birthday present, but I just couldn't let it go. Later that evening, I started talking with my mom about what I could get this boy as a token of my appreciation for his friendship. She saw through it, though, and pointed out what I was up to. I was trying to appease my guilty conscience by giving something back to him, something that would lessen the feeling that I owed him something. I was trying to pay for the gift. In the end, she just smiled and said, "Eric, when someone gives you something wonderful, the best way to respond is to accept it and say thank you."

Jesus's death on the cross is the greatest gift ever given, and it was given to completely undeserving people – you and me. It wasn't something that we earned. It's not like God said, "Wow, they really are trying hard, so I'll help them out a little." Paul points out that just the opposite is true: "While we were still sinners, Christ died for us" (Romans 5:8). While we were still steeped in our rebellion against Him, He stepped across the chasm and established a way for us to be reconciled to Him. Why? Because He loves us and desires to be in relationship with us. Though we are beat up and tarnished, we are still His image-bearers and He was not willing to turn His back on us. Instead, He made a way for us to be restored.

Yes, our natural impulse is to do something to lessen the audacity of His gift. We want to pay Him back in some way. But the whole point of a gift is that it's undeserved and unearned. Paul put it this way: "It is by grace you have been saved, through faith… not by works, so that no one can boast" (Ephesians 2:8-9). We are unworthy of Jesus's death, we are undeserving of the gift of new life, but that's what makes it a truly wonderful gift.

So I encourage you to simply accept His gift and say, "thank you."

Two Pathways

We have before us two pathways, two approaches to dealing with our sin. One way is composed of rules and restrictions, and it depends upon our own efforts. The other pathway is toward the cross, upon which our sins have been nailed. It's a pathway of relationship rather than religion. It's a pathway of grace rather than good works. It's a pathway of submission rather than self-reliance. And according to the Bible, it's the only pathway that will have any effect. We can't heal ourselves - only God can do that. We can't clean ourselves up - only God can do that. So stop trying to do it by your own strength. Stop looking to the "thou shall not's" to save you. They were never meant to do that. Their purpose was simply to lead you to the only one who can: Jesus, our Savior and our Lord.

This is the good news of the cross: that which we were unable to do for ourselves, God has done for us. Through Jesus Christ, He has made perfect forever those who are being made holy. Our Creator makes old and battered things new.

Taking the First Step

Before we move on, there is one aspect of grace that I want to clarify - Jesus didn't just die on the cross so that our sins could be forgiven. That was a means to an end. His true purpose in dying was to restore mankind's relationship with Him – a relationship that was lost when Adam and Eve took that first disobedient bite. Jesus died so that we can come out of hiding and be reunited with our Creator. He died to purchase us out of slavery to sin, so that we can follow Him on an adventure of a lifetime.

Time and again, Jesus presented people with the same invitation: "Follow me." He invited them to leave the life they knew to join him in what he was doing. He invited them to walk with him, learn from him, and work alongside of him. And because of the cross, you and I have the same opportunity – we can follow Jesus, both in this life and into eternity.

As the saying goes, "A journey of a thousand miles begins with a single step." And so it is with this invitation to follow Jesus. The first step is simply to accept the gift of grace that he purchased for you on the cross.

If you recognize your need for God's grace and you want to answer Jesus's invitation to follow him, then I encourage you to pray this simple prayer (or one like it).[28]

God, I confess that I am a sinner and that my sin separates me from you. But I also recognize that you love me in spite of my sin and that you sent Jesus to die for me so that I can live with you. Jesus, thank you for dying for me. I accept the gift of grace that you purchased for me on the cross, and I invite you to be the Lord of my life. Please come into my heart and begin to clean house. I want to follow you, so please help me to relinquish control of my life to you, my Savior and my Lord. Amen.

If you just prayed this prayer for the first time, don't keep it a secret. Tell another believer. In fact, tell me! I'd love to celebrate with you and help you take some next steps in this adventure called following Jesus. You can reach me by email (ericdwayman@gmail.com). I look forward to hearing from you.

Think About It -

- What are some of the ways you have sinned and fallen short of God's holy standard?

- Why is sin such a big deal? Why does it separate us from God?

- When we are confronted with our sin, one human response is to try and make up for it by fixating on the rules. Yet, God's law was never intended to form a ladder that we could climb to attain righteousness. What was the purpose of the law?

- When we are confronted with the gravity of our sin, we begin to recognize why the Gospel of Jesus Christ is such good news. But what is the Gospel? Read back over the numerous articulations of it found in this chapter, then describe the Good News in your own words.

- Have you accepted God's gift of grace, which Jesus purchased for you on the cross? If not, is there anything keeping you from doing so?

CHAPTER 8

You Are Not Alone

The God of the universe is not something we can just
add to our lives and keep on as we did before.
— Francis Chan, *Forgotten God*

Seven hundred years ago in the region we now call Belgium there lived a man named Duke Raynald III. History doesn't remember much of Raynald's life except for this one point: he was a total glutton. He loved to eat. We might say that food was his drug of choice. When things were going well, he ate. And when things got stressful, he ate. Naturally, because of his large appetite, the Duke's girth followed suit. People mockingly nicknamed him *Crassus* - "Fatty." Today we would simply call him obese.

Duke Raynald had a younger brother named Edward who didn't respect his big brother very much. One day, these siblings got in a fight that escalated into all-out war. In the end, Edward deposed Raynald, forcibly taking the Dukedom from him. But in a departure from fourteenth-century medieval custom, Edward didn't actually kill his older brother. Instead, he imprisoned him in a room in the middle of the castle. But this was unlike any prison cell we would ever expect. There were no locks on the doors or bars on the windows. Raynald could walk out at any time, except for one big problem: with his immense girth, he couldn't fit through the door.

Edward promised that the day Raynald could actually walk out of his prison cell, he would regain his title and all his property. However, this wasn't Edward's way of helping his big brother lose weight. Edward knew his big brother's appetite and saw this as a way to further humiliate Raynald. So every day, Edward had the castle cooks prepare sumptuous feasts which they placed before the captive. At first Raynald resisted the temptation, knowing that each guilty mouthful prolonged his captivity. But his appetite was strong and before long he began to gorge himself. Ironically, despite the fact that moderation was the key to his freedom, Raynald actually began to gain weight.

When someone would accuse Edward of cruelty, he would simply reply: "My brother is not a prisoner; he may leave when he so wills." [29] Yet, Raynald was a prisoner and he lived out the majority of his natural life in that cell – a prisoner of his own appetite.

New Creations, Old Habits

Can you identify with Duke Raynald's story? You turn to something in your life for comfort, perhaps something that promised control, but over time you begin to recognize that it, not you, is actually in control. In his letter to the Romans, Paul states that we are slaves to whomever we obey, whether to God or our gut. The more that we give into our appetites, the more influence our appetites have over our choices. Maybe your thing isn't food. Perhaps it's alcohol, pornography, expanding your bank account, looking good, pursuing success (or at least the appearance of success). Whatever form our jailer takes, many of us are imprisoned by our appetites and don't know how to get free.

Sure, we hear that we are "new creations," but our old habits keep coming back to haunt us. We hear that in Christ we are forgiven and that he has set us free, but we don't feel free. And we can't even forgive ourselves, let alone accept God's forgiveness. So we sit, day after day, year after year, in our own forced captivity, surrounded by shame and guilt, yet unable to walk out that door into the freedom and forgiveness that Christ bought for us on the cross.

This is the paradox of the cross: Jesus died in our place, paying the penalty for our sins and justifying us in the eyes of the law. Therefore, we are rightfully called "new creations." However, God's grace alone does not fully fix our inclination to sin. We are still drawn to it like pigs to mud. The author of Hebrews recognized this two-fold reality when he acknowledged that with Jesus's sacrifice, God "has made perfect forever those who are being made holy." (Hebrews 10:14). By Jesus's death on the cross, we have been justified once and for all. But all of us are still in the process of being made holy; we are still in the process of being set apart from the things that hurt us and dishonor God.

Theologians call this "sanctification" and it's a process that will continue in every Christ-follower throughout their entire life. Even Paul, that giant of the Christian faith, recognized his propensity to sin. He lamented that "I don't really understand myself, for I want to do what is right, but I don't do it. Instead, I do what I hate" (Romans 7: 15 NLT). So how can we be holy when our flesh just won't die?

Some of us figure we just need to try harder and gut it out. After all, God helps those who help themselves, right?! Actually, this statement is found nowhere in scripture, but that doesn't stop us from living like it's the gospel truth.

As we have already seen, many of us, when faced with our depravity, will rely upon our own efforts to clean ourselves up. We may accept that we are saved by grace through faith, but the moralizer in each of us still isn't gone. It's still in there, looking for the part we have to play. Suddenly, it recognizes that we still struggle with sin and it declares, "We must try harder!!!" The only problem is, we are a lot like Duke Raynald, whether we want to admit it or not. When we rely upon our own strength to make ourselves holy, we will fail. Though we may resist the hungers of our flesh for a time, we will eventually find ourselves diving headlong into the very things that separated us from God in the first place.

Still, we are drawn to the belief that we must do it on our own. So, just as we did when we tried to earn our righteousness, we try and use rules and regulations to help us become holy. Rules are a tempting substitute for intimacy with Christ, because they are black and white, right or wrong, and they give us the false impression that our holiness is something we can control. In reality, however, they can't make us holy any more than they could put us into right standing with God.

The Apostle Paul recognized this fact. He admitted that "such regulations indeed have an appearance of wisdom, with their self-imposed worship, their false humility and their harsh treatment of the body, but they lack any value in restraining sensual indulgence" (Colossians 2:23). For those of us who are sick of stumbling in our sin over and over again, rules and thou-shalt-not's are pretty attractive. They give the appearance of wisdom and the illusion of control. They may even help us achieve a momentary victory over our sinful habits. But they lack any lasting value in restraining sensual indulgence; they simply do not have the power to help us grow. What's worse, when we fixate on our own efforts to make ourselves holy, we actually take our eyes off of the only one who can help.

It's like the time that Peter got out of the boat and began to walk toward Jesus on the water. He wasn't keeping himself afloat, Jesus was. Then all of a sudden, his attention was drawn away from his Lord and onto the wind and the waves. He began to think, "I can't do this," and he was absolutely right. In that moment he began to sink, because he was utterly unable to follow in Jesus's footsteps by his own strength. When his attention was on Jesus, it was Jesus who held him above the water, but when he took his attention off of Jesus and onto his own abilities to keep himself afloat, he got wet.

Ironically, the more we fixate on the rules and try to fix ourselves through willpower alone, the greater our awareness of our sinful nature will become. A couple years ago, I was walking in the mountains during a warm summer evening. It was dark out and there was only one street light on the road I was walking down. As I passed under the light and continued beyond it, I suddenly noticed my shadow at my feet. With each step away from the light, my shadow grew and grew until it was massive, towering in front of me and completely eclipsing the light. But as I turned and began to walk back up that same street, toward the light, my shadow fell behind me. It was still there of course, but I wasn't focused on it anymore. Rather, I was focused on the light. And with each step closer to the source of the light, my shadow grew smaller and smaller. Though it never disappeared altogether, it certainly became less apparent.

I think that's a perfect metaphor for how the sanctification process works. While our human nature tells us that we need to go clean ourselves up before we come to Jesus, the message of the gospel cries out for just the opposite response: run to Jesus and allow Him to clean us up. Rules don't make us stop sinning; they just increase the guilt. Christ alone can help us outgrow our sin. Only He can fill those deep-rooted areas of our heart that we have been futilely trying to satiate through things like food, alcohol, lust, climbing the corporate ladder, accumulation, dating or anything else. Christ alone can satisfy the hunger of our heart. It's like the old hymn declares:

> *Turn your eyes upon Jesus,*
> *look full in his wonderful face,*
> *and the things of earth will grow strangely dim*
> *in the light of his glory and grace.*[30]

A Brief Clarification

Based upon the previous section, it would seem that the answer is to simply focus on Jesus and pursue him. However, this approach still puts the responsibility squarely upon our shoulders. And we have already seen what happens when we rely upon our own strength – we inevitably fail. So how do we embrace the gift of freedom that Christ bought for us on the cross? How do we take the steps to walk out the door of our self-imposed prison cells?

Trying to fix ourselves through our own efforts is futile. We simply cannot do it, as Raynald can attest. Maybe the answer is to rely completely on God to do the transformation. Yet, if we go too far in that direction, we end up making no effort at all; we just sit in our sin and cry out, "God, change me!"

In reality, neither of these extremes is true; we have a part to play in our own sanctification, but we cannot do it by ourselves. In his letter to the church in Philippi, Paul exhorts Christ-followers to *"continue to work out your salvation* with fear and trembling, for *it is God who works in you* to will and to act in order to fulfill his good purpose"(Philippians 2:12-13, emphasis added).

Paul recognized that we have a part to play in the process of being sanctified. We need to continually work out our salvation, day in and day out. However, we cannot do this on our own. Thankfully, God doesn't expect us to. He is right there with us, working in and through us to both desire and carry out His will for our lives.

God With Us

There is something truly comforting about knowing that we are not stumbling through life alone, that our God is with us. Even though our Creator transcends both time and space, He stays intimately involved in the lives of His people. The Israelites experienced this powerfully as God led them out of slavery and into the Promised

Land. Early on in the journey, He commissioned a Tabernacle (a tent of meeting) where the people could come and meet with Him. From that point forward, whenever the chosen people of God stopped for the night, this Tabernacle was set up first, at the very center of the campsite, and the rest of the tribes would arrange themselves around it. The Tabernacle became a tangible reminder that their God was with them, residing in their midst.

Later on, when Israel took possession of the Promised Land and settled down to enjoy God's provision, God instructed them to build the Temple, which was simply a more permanent tabernacle in the heart of the nation's capital, Jerusalem. Once again, the Temple was a tangible reminder of God's presence with His people. He was not far off and inaccessible. He was in their midst and the Israelites would regularly come to the Temple in Jerusalem in order to worship and commune with Him. Still, this wasn't close enough for God.

In John 1, we are told that Jesus, the incarnate Word of God who had been so instrumental in creation, "took on flesh and made his dwelling among us" (John 1:14). Interestingly, the word that we translate "made his dwelling" is the same Greek word that was used to translate the Hebrew word "tabernacle." Therefore, we could just as easily translate this verse: "The Word became flesh and tabernacled among us." Both the Tabernacle and the Temple were prototypes for what was to come – God residing in the midst of His people in the form of His one and only son. Jesus was the physical embodiment of the Tabernacle, the true Temple of God in their midst. That's why, when the Pharisees questioned Jesus's authority, he told them, "destroy this temple, and I will raise it again in three days" (John 2:19). He wasn't talking about the building in Jerusalem. He was talking about himself.

Of course, Jesus isn't walking among us in the flesh any longer. After he rose from the grave on that first Easter morning and then spent some time preparing his disciples, he ascended into heaven where he now sits in the true throne-room of God, the place which both the Tabernacle and Temple were modeled after. So does that mean God is no longer among us? Thankfully, the answer is a resounding, No! Our God is still in our midst. In fact, He is closer than we could imagine.

Temples of the Living God

During the last meal Jesus shared with his disciples prior to his crucifixion, he comforted them with the assurance that he wouldn't leave them (or us) alone. He told them, "I will ask my Father and he will give you another advocate to help you and be with you forever – the Spirit of Truth … You know him, for *he lives with you* and *will be in you.*" (John 14:16-17, emphasis added)

This Advocate[31] is God's Holy Spirit, and He is given as God's stamp of ownership and empowerment to anyone who places their faith in Jesus Christ. The Holy Spirit acts as our comforter, our counselor, and our guide who comes alongside of us as we seek to follow Jesus. He enables us to submit to God's guidance, giving us strength to say no to the cries of our flesh. It is the Holy Spirit who joins us in the sanctification process, helping us in our weakness. So when Paul says in Philippians 2:13 that "it is God who works in you to will and to act in order to fulfill his good purpose," he is speaking of God's Spirit working within us. But that's not even the best part.

What is truly remarkable is that with the giving of His Spirit, God doesn't merely reside near us - He resides within us! That means we are not merely New Creations; we are quite literally temples of God, where His Spirit lives! Paul recognized this fact and pointed out the gravity of this truth in his first letter to the Corinthians. He exclaimed, "Do you not know that your bodies are temples of the Holy Spirit, who is in you, whom you have received from God? You are not your own; you were bought at a price. Therefore honor God with your bodies" (1 Corinthians 6:19-20).

You may be thinking, "Ok, but why does any of this matter?" The truth that God resides within us affects everything, from how we live to how we relate to God and one another.

For instance, it ought to compel us to reconsider how we live our lives. At one point in Israel's history, God's Spirit departed from the Temple in Jerusalem because of the rampant immorality and idolatry that the Israelites had allowed to take place in it.[32] Now, we might shake our heads at those foolish Israelites, but stop and consider this: We are now the temples of God. What sort of images and messages do we allow into our lives? What sort of unholy things do we consume? In what ways do we treat our bodies, God's temple, with contempt, using and abusing it in ways that disrespect its rightful owner? In what ways have we spoken hateful words of condemnation over our bodies? May I simply remind you, as Paul has, that "you are not your own. You were bought at a price. Therefore, honor God with your body."

Furthermore, the realization that God is with us could also alter the way we connect with Him. We don't need to have a pastor or priest intercede for us. We have direct access to the Creator and Sustainer of the Universe. When Jesus was crucified, the curtain in the temple that had separated God's people from the Holy of Holies was torn in two, from top to bottom.[33] This curtain had protected God's throne on earth, the Ark of the Covenant, from being profaned by the sins of the people. By tearing the veil, God was declaring, "You no longer need to stay far from me. You can come directly to me, just as you are. You can bring your questions, your fears, your hopes and your needs directly to Me." The truly remarkable thing about our God is that He doesn't view our desire for relationship as a nuisance. He loves us and longs to spend time with us as well. That's the whole reason Jesus suffered and died in the first place.

Similarly, the message that God is with us can transform the ways in which we approach difficult times in our lives. When we walk through a painful or scary season, it's easy to feel utterly alone. When we find ourselves in the valley of the shadow of death, it can feel as if God has completely abandoned us. But the Bible reminds us that God is still with us even in those painful times. It's just that sometimes our fears, our frustrations or our self-sufficiency can cloud our ability to see God in the midst of our struggles. In those times, perhaps the best way to pray is to be honest about our need for Him: "God, I know that you're here in this. Help me to see your face." After all, prayer isn't a time to pretend to have it all together; it's a time to be honest with the only one who is in control.

What's more, the fact that God is with us doesn't just impact the way we live our lives. It can and should cause us to rethink the way we share our faith with others. Many of us have family, friends and neighbors that we pray will come to know Jesus and we plot and scheme, looking for some way to get them to step foot into church, as if that's the only place they might meet Him. The reality is that they don't need to enter a church building to be in the presence of God. We carry Him within us everywhere we go and the way we interact with them, speak to them and live our lives in front of them speaks more loudly and is more compelling than anything a pastor could say to them from the pulpit. Our lives may be the only gospel that some people read. So what is your life saying about our God?

Think About It –

- Can you identity with the story of Duke Reynald? What appetites tend to keep you imprisoned?

- How have you gone about battling these appetites? What has worked? What hasn't?

- The Apostle Paul told believers, "continue to work out your salvation with fear and trembling, for it is God who works in you to will and to act in order to fulfill his good purpose"(Philippians

2:12-13). In what ways is the sanctification process a partnership between God and us?

- Why can't we do it all on our own? Why can't God do it for us without any effort on our part?

- What is God's purpose for giving us His Holy Spirit to reside within us?

- How might the realization that God's Spirit is with you affect the way you go through your day?

- In what ways does it encourage you?

- In what ways does it convict you?

CHAPTER 9

Part of the Family

I was once an orphan with no hope, with no purpose, no aim;
but God in his kindness saw me and adopted me into His family,
changed my past, changed my future, changed everything about me.
—Aaron Ivey[34]

In the game of life, Sammy was dealt a difficult hand. He was born
to a poor, single mother in Ghana and the fact that he was even
given a chance to live was a testament to both his mother's love for
him as well as her trust in God. She already had a six-year-old son,
so when she became pregnant with Sammy, the father declared that
if she was unwilling to get an abortion he would leave her. Since
this man was her only source of income, she recognized the choice
set before her: security for her and her older son or a chance at life
for her unborn child. In the end, she simply could not bring herself
to end Sammy's life. So she refused to abort him and, true to his
word, the father left them to fend for themselves.

Sammy's mother ended up moving in with her mother and
grandmother, who ran a small street kiosk. She joined them in
selling their trinkets so that she could buy enough food to feed her
little family. On a good day, she might earn a single dollar, which
was all they would have to live on. This kiosk where she worked
was also where they lived, a 4'X6' wooden box with no furniture,

no running water, and no bathroom. It would be uncomfortable for a lone adult, but three grown women and a six-year-old boy called it home. And soon a newborn baby was to join them.

Shortly after Sammy's birth, Ghana's social services found out about the conditions he was being raised in and gave his mother an ultimatum – either increase your daily income dramatically or give him up for adoption. They argued that to try and raise him under the current circumstances would be child endangerment. But as a street peddler, there was simply no way that she could make enough to properly care for both boys. So a year after he was born, Sammy's mother made a horrendously difficult decision and gave him up for adoption.

Around this time, half a world away, God was beginning to plant a new vision in a young couple's heart. Jesse and Brandi Gibbs had recently given birth to their first child, a daughter named Adalee. Then one day as Brandi was praying, she had a vision of a young, dark skinned boy running up to her, throwing his arms around her neck and calling her "mommy." Suddenly, a thought began to take root in her heart: "What if God has a son for us somewhere out there?" She shared the thought with Jesse and together they began to pray, "God, if it is your will for us to adopt, please open the right doors and lead us to the child you have for us." And they waited for an answer.

As time passed, the conviction that there was another child out there that belonged in their family grew in intensity and they began to seriously look into the adoption process. Eventually, through a long, winding path that was saturated with prayer and marked by a number of serendipitous circumstances, God led Brandi and Jesse to Sammy. They were certain this was the boy God had broken their hearts to find, so they began the long, costly and emotionally-consuming process of adopting him into their family.

After many long months of court dates, long distance phone calls and countless prayers, Sammy officially became a member of the Gibbs family and Brandi flew to Ghana one last time to bring her son home. I was at the airport the day Sammy came home to live with his new family. It was an emotional celebration for all of us who had been anticipating this day for so long. But Sammy seemed a bit bewildered by all of it. After all, he was barely two years old. This little boy had no idea of the time, the sacrifices and the cost that his new mom and dad had gone to in order to make him their son. He had no clue how many people had contributed to their endeavor, both prayerfully and financially. He couldn't even grasp the gravity of what was taking place there at the Los Angeles Airport baggage claim: he was being welcomed into his new family. He was coming home for the very first time.

Sons and Daughters of God

Sammy's transition from orphan to adopted son is a lot like the transition new believers take when they place their faith in Jesus Christ and accept him as their Savior and Lord. Through Christ, we become sons and daughters of God.

You might be thinking, "Hasn't God always been my Father?" Actually, no. Now, it is true that we were all created by God and bear His image, albeit imperfectly. However, sin separated us from Him. From the moment Adam and Eve took that first bite and disobeyed God, sin severed the union mankind had with our Creator and enslaved us. So we are born into captivity, sold into slavery by the choices of our ancestors.[35] We can't really blame them for our predicament, though, since we are just as inclined to sin as they were.

However, in spite of our chains we are no ordinary slaves. We are the descendants of royalty. We bear a striking resemblance to the King of Creation, though any similarity is obscured by the grimy residue of our bondage. Nor does our royal ancestry give us any claim to the throne. We are slaves and that is all there is to it. But then one day our King showed up and bought us out of slavery, paying the blood debt that hung over our heads and kept us in chains. Because of what he's done for us, we no longer have to remain in captivity under sin's harsh control; we can now belong to the King if we are willing to accept His gift of grace through faith. We have been bought at a steep price, but it was one He was willing to pay. That, in and of itself, is wonderful news, but our King doesn't stop there!

When we accept the gift, He then declares that He is adopting us into His royal family. From that moment forward, we are no longer slaves; we are now children of the King. The old has gone, the new has come. This is the amazing reality of the cross. This is the extravagance of God's love for us, that we should be called His children![36]

The means by which God makes us His children is worth exploring. In the last chapter, we saw the way that God draws near to those of us who have given our hearts to Him and accepted His gift of grace. He literally fills us with His Holy Spirit as both His seal of ownership[37] and His way of helping us begin the sanctification process. However, there is another massive implication of the Spirit's presence in our lives that is often overlooked.

Right in the middle of his letter to the Romans, Paul exclaims that "those who are led by the Spirit of God are the children of God. The Spirit you received does not make you slaves, so that you live in fear again; rather the Spirit you received brought about your adoption to sonship. And by him we cry, 'Abba, Father.' The Spirit himself testifies with our spirit that we are God's children" (Romans 8:14-16).

Did you catch that? It is through the Holy Spirit that we become adopted into the family of God. Because of the Spirit's presence in our lives, we do not need to cower in the King's presence like a slave. Rather, like a son or daughter, we can approach Him with confidence that we are accepted and loved. Furthermore, we don't need to speak to Him in formal language, like a servant would. Instead, we can talk to Him like Jesus did, with terms of intimacy. Jesus called the Father *Abba*, which is Aramaic for "daddy." It is without a doubt the single most intimate name of God found anywhere in the Bible, a name that only His true child would call Him. And because of the Spirit's presence in our lives we also have the right to call God our *Abba,* our Daddy.

I think of Sammy walking up to Jesse in the airport. Though he didn't know Jesse nearly as well as his new sister Adalee did, Sammy had just as much right to call him Daddy as she did. Because of his adoption, he was a rightful part of the family.

A Deeper Look at Adoption

Through the Holy Spirit, we are adopted into God's family, making the Creator and Sustainer of the Universe our Father. This is a big deal no matter how you look at it. But keep in mind that when Paul wrote that "the Spirit you received brought about your adoption to sonship" (Romans 8:15), he was writing to Christ-followers living in Rome during the first century. They would have had a radically different understanding of what it meant to be adopted than we do. So let's take a bit of a detour into history and see if we can uncover the true implications of our spiritual adoption.

In the first century, Jews did not practice legal adoption, so Paul is most likely using the Greco-Roman practice as his model.[38] This conclusion is supported by the fact that he is writing to a Roman audience who would have seen a number of public adoption proceedings.[39] That said, the Greco-Roman custom of legal adoption had a very different focus than our modern ones. Today, families typically adopt young children in order to care for them until they grow into adults. In contrast, Roman adoptions were far more focused on continuing the family name and ensuring that there was someone to inherit the family estate. If a Roman family had no male heir, their possessions and their name were in danger of being lost. So they would adopt an heir who was usually a fully grown adult. William Barclay lays out four of the most important legal changes that would take place during a Roman adoption:

1) The adopted person lost all rights in his old family and gained all the rights of a legitimate son in his new family. In the most binding legal way, he got a new father.

2) It followed that he became heir to his new father's estate. Even if other sons were afterwards born, it did not affect his rights. He was inalienably co-heir with them.

3) By law, the old life of the adopted person was completely wiped out; for instance, all debts were cancelled. He was regarded as a new person entering into a new life with which the past had nothing to do.

4) In the eyes of the law, he was absolutely the son of his new father. [40]

Can you see why Paul would use this metaphor to describe our new standing with the Father? Through the impartation of the Spirit and the atonement of the cross, we have become new creations. Our old self, with its massive sin-debt, is no more and through Christ we become a new person who can rightfully call God our Father. Because of this, we become co-heirs of eternal life with Jesus, God's only begotten (natural, not adopted) son. Paul himself made this point in Romans 8:17, declaring that "if we are children, then we are heirs – heirs of God and co-heirs with Christ."

If we dig a little deeper, the Roman custom of adoption has one more massive implication that simply cannot be overlooked. According to Roman law, a father could disown his natural born children for any reason. In fact, history tells us that when a Roman baby was born, the nursemaid would lay the newborn child at the father's feet. If he stooped to pick it up, that child was accepted into the family, but if he turned his back, the baby was taken out of the house and left to die. This practice was called exposure, since the baby was exposed to the elements. One letter, written by a husband who was away on business to his pregnant wife illustrates just how common and accepted this practice was in the First Century Roman world:

*Heartiest greetings...Do not worry if I must remain in
Alexandria when the others return. I beg and beseech
you to take care of the little child. As soon as I receive
wages I will send them to you. If, with luck, you have a
child and it is a boy, let it live. If it is a girl, throw it out.
You told Aphrodisia to tell me, "Do not forget me." How
could I forget you? I beg you not to worry.*[41]

It's shocking to hear the offhanded way in which this father-to-be speaks of rejecting his unborn child as if it's moldy bread. We wouldn't even treat an unwanted pet with this much disregard. Yet this was the reality of the Roman world. Life was treated lightly and a child's position in the home was tenuous at best. Even a fully grown child could be disowned by the father if he or she displeased him.

Yet, this brings us to the most important implication of Roman adoption: Though a Roman citizen could disown his own naturally born children, by law he could never disown his adopted child.[42] In other words, once adopted, this person could *never* be unadopted!

Consider the implications of that statement for a moment: With the impartation of God's Spirit within us, we are completely and utterly secure. Nothing and nobody can take our identity as God's children from us. This realization led Paul to exclaim:

> I am convinced that nothing can ever separate us
> from God's love. Neither death nor life, neither
> angels nor demons, neither our fears for today nor
> our worries about tomorrow—not even the powers
> of hell can separate us from God's love. No power
> in the sky above or in the earth below—indeed,
> nothing in all creation will ever be able to separate
> us from the love of God that is revealed in Christ
> Jesus our Lord. (Romans 8:38-39 NLT)[43]

Embracing Our New Life in God's Family

Our God has adopted us into His family and called us His sons and daughters. We are secure in our new identity as His children. Of course, this doesn't necessarily mean that we will feel secure.

When Sammy first came home, it wasn't a completely smooth transition. Though he was a fully adopted son, he had a hard time letting go of old habits. For instance, although he was fed three times a day, he began to stash bread rolls from dinner in his bedroom just in case the food stopped coming. This habit, which he'd picked up in the orphanage, revealed the insecurity he felt toward his new position in life. To his young mind, these kind people may have taken him in, but that didn't mean they would always take care of him. So he wasn't ready to let his guard down fully and embrace his new position in the Gibbs family.

Similarly, when we come to Christ, we often have a hard time fully resting in our new identity as sons and daughters of God. Undoubtedly, part of our difficulty stems from our families of origin. We simply cannot help but allow our experiences with our earthly families to influence our perspective on our heavenly family. If we felt loved and secure within our family of origin, then it might not be that difficult to rest in our new role as members of God's family. However, if we experienced insecurity within our families of origin, then we will almost certainly experience the same sense of insecurity with our new identity as sons and daughters of God.

Consider the fact that we call God our Father. This naturally draws parallels to our earthly fathers, for better or worse. Whether we realize we are doing it or not, we begin to view and approach our Heavenly Father with the same posture and attitude we approached our earthly father. Thus, if our dad was a harsh disciplinarian, we will naturally view God as a harsh disciplinarian. If our dad's approval was contingent upon our performance, we will likely view God's approval and love as conditional. And if our biological father was absent from our life, it will be difficult for us to view God as anything other than distant and disinterested in us. We will explore this reality in greater detail in the next chapter; however, it's an important point to recognize here, since our ability to rest in our new identity is inextricably tied to our trust in the one who calls us His sons and daughters.

Author Lee Strobel explains that "faith is only as good as the one in whom it's invested."[44] Throughout our lives we put our faith in imperfect people and often we get hurt, which makes us hesitant to trust the next person. Sammy didn't understand that his mother had given him up for adoption so that he could have a chance at a better life. All he knew was that she was not there for him. In fact, every single person that he bonded with during the first couple years of his life ultimately disappeared from it. It's no wonder why he would have a difficult time trusting in the security of his new family. Yet, his standing wasn't dependent upon his perception, was it? No, it was dependent upon the legal and relational commitment that his new parents had made to him. Despite the fact that he felt uncertain in his circumstances, he was completely secure in his new identity as their son.

In the same way, our standing with God has far more to do with His faithfulness than ours. Our acceptance into His family is neither something we earned nor deserve. It is a gift given to us by our loving Father who created us to be in relationship with Him. He chose to adopt us. So we can stop trying to prove our worthiness and simply live as a member of His family. We can stop hiding from our Heavenly Father every time we stumble in sin as if He is going to disown us; instead, we can run to Him and allow Him to help us overcome our sin nature.

It is by grace we have been saved and by grace we live, though God's grace is not permission to live any way that we want.[45] After all, we are now members of His family and that means we are representing Him. Therefore, as sons and daughters of God, we ought to make it our aim to submit to our heavenly Father's directives, just as Jesus did. Jesus declared that he did nothing on his own, but only what he saw the Father doing (John 5:19). In the same way, we should make every effort to live as children of God. Of course, we can't do this on our own, nor do we need to. We have God's Spirit within us to lead us and enable us to deny the flesh and emulate Jesus, our brother and role model. Jesus said that "whoever does the will of my Father in heaven is my brother and sister" (Matthew 12:50). Of course, as we've discussed in previous chapters, our efforts to be holy as our Father is holy should never be viewed as a prerequisite to our adoption as His children, but rather as a joyful response to it.

One Big Happy Family

On the day of his adoption, Sammy didn't just gain new parents and a new last name. He gained a sister. Similarly, when we are adopted into God's family, we not only gain God as our Father and Jesus as our older brother, we also gain a whole slew of other brothers and sisters who have been adopted by faith into the family of God. It's sobering to consider that every man, woman and child who has ever been saved by faith is our spiritual sibling. We are all part of the same family, even though we may never meet one another this side of eternity.

This means that even though there are thousands of denominations and millions of church gatherings around the globe, there is really only one Church, one family of God and we are all part of it. On the night before Jesus's crucifixion, he actually prayed for the unity of this family who would believe the good news and accept the gift of salvation he was just about to purchase on the cross:

> I pray also for those who will believe in me
> through [the disciples'] message, that all of them
> may be one, Father, just as you are in me and I am

in you. May they also be in us so that the world may believe that you have sent me. I have given them the glory that you gave me, that they may be one as we are one— I in them and you in me—so that they may be brought to complete unity. Then the world will know that you sent me and have loved them even as you have loved me" (John 17:20-23).

Jesus's prayer was for the unity of God's family, which would act as a testimony to the unbelieving world that Jesus really was the Son of God and that he truly does transform lives. Sadly, this isn't really how it plays out. More often than not, it feels like God's family is one big dysfunctional mess.

Far too often, we seek disunity over unity. We openly gossip about the faults and failings of our neighboring church bodies, comparing and competing with one another rather than working together to impact the community with the love of Christ. We steal sheep from one another's flocks, swelling our church's numbers through transfer growth rather than bringing new people to Christ. We get into heated arguments on social media about trivial theological points, rather than focusing on our main point of agreement - that Jesus died for sinners like us so that we could be reconciled to God.

Jesus declared that the world would know we are his disciples by the way we love one another, but all too often our actions show the world that God's family is just as messed up and dysfunctional as their families are. So why would they want to join us?! What is attractive about our petty squabbling and open competition?

Obviously this isn't going to change overnight. However, just because we cannot overcome the problem by ourselves doesn't mean we shouldn't do something to address it. We can start by embracing the fact that, in Christ, we are all brothers and sisters; we are all heirs of the Kingdom of God and we will be spending eternity together. Furthermore, we are all God's representatives and the way we treat one another often speaks far louder than our theological perspectives.

Over the last few years, I have watched as a number of the churches in my community have intentionally stopped competing with one another, choosing instead to work together to impact the community in which we reside. Though we meet in different locations and have different worship styles, we have the same Father God. So we have sought to represent Him and serve the least and the lost in our city together. Believers from a number of different churches regularly gather together to pray for our city. When one church plans an outreach, such as mentoring struggling students in under-performing schools, the opportunity to serve is opened up to the community of church bodies. After all, there is no reason to reinvent the wheel. When tragedy strikes, such as when a city employee committed suicide after receiving a pink slip, the Church gathered around City Hall, joined hands with our city officials and openly prayed for healing and unity for our hurting community.

We still have a long way to go, but we are moving in the right direction. We are seeking to love our community as a unified family, rather than as individual churches. We are addressing some of the most pressing issues that our city is facing - namely homelessness, illiteracy, and immigration - using the combined talents and resources that He has entrusted to our care. And we are beginning to see a change in public perception as a result. In the past, the churches in our city were perceived by our civic leaders as obstacles rather than partners for change. If we did anything to address the issues around us, we did it according to our own opinions of what needed to be done, which were often at odds with what the city was trying to do.

For instance, at one point, our city officials were trying to move the growing homeless population away from a park that had become unsafe for children to play in and encourage them to utilize resource centers that were set up to care for their needs. But a group of well-meaning Christ-followers refused to stop doing daily feedings in the park, even though there was a soup kitchen just down the street that was serving the same function. These believers were fixated on caring for the needy in their midst, which is wonderful, but they were unwilling to change their approach even though it declared to the city that we were unwilling to work together toward a common goal.

Today, the Church in our city is making a concerted effort to work with our civic leaders to address the needs in our community. Take homelessness for instance. We have partnered with the city to establish a homeless consortium made up of people from a number of churches as well as city leaders in order to try to hammer out a viable long-term solution for the homeless in our midst. In the meantime, we have set up some new resources to address the tangible needs of our homeless population. We have established a check-in-center on the campus of one of our larger churches, where the homeless can check in their belongings so that they don't have to cart them around everywhere they go. We have also acquired a mobile laundry and shower facility so that the homeless can wash their clothes and themselves. The check-in-center and mobile facilities are staffed by volunteers from a number of churches throughout our city and no single church's name is attached to it. It is simply a ministry of the Church in Costa Mesa and is operating under the full blessing of our civic leaders.

Though there is still a lot of work to be done, these efforts have radically altered the perception of the unified family of God in our city. We are no longer perceived as primarily disinterested and dysfunctional. We are now a key partner in addressing the biggest problems our city is facing. When an issue comes up, our city officials have begun asking the Church to help, rather than having to work around us. [46]

In short, as adopted sons and daughters of God, we represent our Father, whether we want to or not. People who would never step foot in our churches come face to face with His children and they make a judgement about our Father based upon what they see in us. My prayer is that we represent Him well and that, in partnership with the Holy Spirit, we can work together as a single, unified family to address the things that break our Father's heart.

Think About It –

- Read Romans 8:14-17. What role does the Holy Spirit play in our adoption?

- How does our adoption affect the way we can approach our Heavenly Father?

- Is it easy for you to rest in your identity as a son or daughter of God? Why or why not?

- In this chapter we explored some distinct characteristics of Roman adoptions that influence the way we understand our own spiritual adoption. Which of those characteristics stand out the most? Why?

- How might your attitude and approach to other Christians change if you embraced the fact that they are your brother or sister in Christ?

CHAPTER 10

Secure in the Father's Love

You are my son, whom I love; with you I am well pleased.
- Mark 1:11

Ted Turner is one of the most successful entrepreneurs in history. He took his father's billboard advertising agency and built it into a media empire, becoming a billionaire and one of the largest private landholders in America in the process. Yet, Turner's successes were driven by a deep-seated insecurity that can clearly be traced back to his relationship with his father, Edward "Ed" Turner, Sr.

Ed Turner was a successful businessman himself, but his work kept him away from home a great deal. When he was there, he was often drunk and would get physically abusive with his only son and namesake, Edward "Ted" Turner, Jr. He figured he was just trying to beat some sense into the boy. When that didn't work, he shipped Ted off to a boarding school and then on to a military academy. Ted's dad also tended to withhold his affection from his son, greeting him with a handshake rather than a hug. All of this was part of the elder Turner's attempt to instill a little insecurity into his boy. As Ted would later recall, his father was driven by the belief "that people who were insecure worked harder."[47]

Ed Turner was also famously outspoken when it came to criticizing his son's choices. When Ted declared that he wanted to study Classic Literature in college, rather than get a business degree, his dad wrote him a scathing letter, declaring that "I am appalled, even horrified, that you have adopted Classics as a major. As a matter of fact, I almost puked on the way home today... I think you are rapidly becoming a jackass, and the sooner you get out of that filthy atmosphere, the better it will suit me."[48] In the end, the pressure of his father's disapproval compelled Ted to switch his major to economics.

Eventually, Ted went to work for his dad in his advertising agency, but the pressure to perform only increased. Ed rode his son mercilessly, using that time to further shape and mold his boy into the man he wanted him to be. Ted worked under the heavy shadow of his father for several years until Ed Turner, who was tormented by insecurity of his own, committed suicide.

Almost twenty years later, at a commencement speech at Georgetown University, Ted admitted that his father's death left him adrift in the world. "It left me alone, because I had counted on him to make the judgement of whether or not I was a success."[49] In another speech a year earlier, Ted, who was already considered to be one of the most successful entrepreneurs of his generation, pulled out a copy of Success Magazine which had his picture on the cover and held it up over his head. "Turning his eyes toward the ceiling, Ted whispered, 'Is this enough for you, Dad?' "[50]

Despite all of his achievements, despite all of the accolades he'd received, Ted Turner was haunted by the shadow of his father's disapproval. He was driven by the question, "Is my dad proud of me?" and no amount of success could shake the feeling that in his father's eyes the answer was "No."

In Search of Our Father's Blessing

I want you to think about your own father for a moment, the man whose blood courses through your veins. Regardless of whether this man knew how to be a father, he has had a profound impact on your life, hasn't he? Even if he wasn't around at all, his presence - or lack thereof - still casts a shadow over your early life.

Our dads have a God-given responsibility to name us. I don't just mean the name on your birth certificate, though that is certainly part of our identity. Our fathers shape our self-image during the most formative years of our lives, when we are still learning about the world and finding our place in it. It is our parents, and our fathers in particular, who shape the way we view ourselves and the world around us. A father's words carry a weight that far exceeds that of other adults in our lives. And these words can be either a blessing or a curse.

For Ted, his father's words became the impetus for his frantic climb up the ladder of accomplishment. We might be tempted to label his dad's influence a blessing, since Ted may never have achieved the same level of success had it not been for the insecurity instilled in him by his dad. However, every aspect of Ted's life has been overshadowed by the curse of that insecurity. His drive to achieve was driven by the fear of his father's disapproval. Even his success was tainted by the troubling belief that it wasn't enough. So he could never rest, never stop climbing; his life was haunted by the shadow of his dad's displeasure. And in the process of earning the blessing of a man who was no longer around to give it to him, he sacrificed the blessing of relationships with the people in his life who were: his three ex-wives and five children. In the end, Ed Turner conferred upon his son an insatiable drive for achievement and an inability to rest in his identity. Though Ted's bank account may suggest that his dad's influence was a blessing, the collateral damage on his life seems to suggest otherwise.

Like Ted, we all want the blessing of our father, the confirmation that we are enough and that we are secure in his love. But not every father knows how to give this blessing to their children. It's not that they don't love their kids; far from it. I've never met a father who didn't love his children, but I've met plenty of guys who didn't know how to speak into the light what they felt in their hearts. Honestly, many fathers never learned how to do it, because they never had it modeled for them. And I've met plenty of amazing kids whose fathers weren't around at all. Yet, just because their dads were absent didn't mean these kids stopped yearning for their father's blessing. If anything, it only magnified their need for acceptance.

When we don't get our father's blessing, either because he doesn't know how to impart it or he isn't around to give it to us, then we will naturally go looking for someone else to fill that need. We will strap on our "validate me" sign and go in search of someone else who can tell us we are worthy. We will end up seeking the blessing from our bosses, our peers or our significant others and we will do just about anything to get it. Girls will give their bodies away in exchange for the security of knowing they are loved. Boys will endure the physical pain of being "jumped in" to a gang, because the yearning for acceptance and belonging is far stronger than their aversion to being hurt. We will sacrifice time, energy, even our convictions - all in the name of obtaining the blessing that our fathers should have given us. Yet, these secondary blessings are never enough, are they? They never truly quench the aching feeling inside that we just don't measure up.

So what's the alternative?

Resting in the Father's Blessing

If we call Jesus our Lord and Savior, then it makes sense to look to him for direction. And even a cursory glance through any of the four gospels will reveal a striking difference between Jesus's approach to life and ours. He wasn't driven by a frantic need to prove his worth. He wasn't a social chameleon who adapted his habits or his message to fit in with the people around him. The scriptures reveal that Jesus simply wasn't concerned about the opinions of his peers or the power-brokers of his day.

Time and again, he seemed to do what he was going to do, regardless of whether or not it was socially acceptable. He ate with sinners and tax collectors, touched lepers, and allowed harlots to wash his feet even though it caused the religious elite to scoff. Jesus wasn't only immune to ridicule and conflict, though. He was equally immune to public acclaim.

At one point, Jesus miraculously turned a young boy's lunch into a feast for a multitude. As the crowds filled their stomachs, they remembered another time God had provided food for His people in the wilderness as He led them out of slavery and toward the Promised Land. Suddenly, a revolutionary thought began to spread throughout the gathered masses: "This Jesus could be the long-awaited Messiah, the one our God has promised to send in order to redeem us from our enemies." And they began to whisper about making him king.

However, Jesus didn't try to fan their excitement, because he knew just how fickle and fleeting social enthusiasm can be. Sure, in that moment this mass of people wanted to storm Herod's palace and make him king by force, but they could just as easily turn on him and call for his crucifixion. So in the end, Jesus just collected his disciples and moved to a different part of the lake in order to minister to more people. But the crowd caught wind of where he had gone and they followed him.

When the people caught up to him, Jesus confronted them about their motives. "You're not hungry for my teaching," he suggested. "Rather, you're after another free lunch." Then he explained that God had sent him from heaven to be the true bread of life that would nourish them for all eternity. He went on to suggest that if they ate of his flesh and drank of his blood, they would never die.

The people were understandably confused. Wasn't he the son of a carpenter? How could he claim to be from God? And what did he mean by suggesting that they needed to eat his flesh and drink his blood? This was a hard teaching.

Now, at this point, if Jesus's ultimate goal was to build a following, he should have backed away from his claim or at least softened it in some way. Perhaps he should have explained that he was speaking metaphorically. However, Jesus did just the opposite - he pressed into the area of their greatest discomfort. He doubled down. So "from that time many of his disciples turned back and no longer followed him" (John 6:66).

Jesus wasn't concerned with public acclaim; he wasn't pandering to an audience of his peers. He didn't even seem all that concerned when most of his disciples started to walk away, confused and disappointed in him.

How could he be so comfortable in the face of rejection? How could he stand by as people who had called themselves his followers rejected him? Furthermore, how could he resist the temptation to pander to the crowds and fan their revolutionary fervor? I'd suggest that it was because Jesus knew who he was, and he knew whose opinion really mattered.

You see, at the very beginning of Jesus's ministry, he was baptized by his cousin John and what transpired during that baptism was foundational to everything that happened afterward. Mark's gospel tells us that "just as Jesus was coming up out of the water, he saw heaven being torn open and the Spirit descending on him like a dove. And a voice came from heaven: 'You are my son, whom I love; with you I am well pleased' " (Mark 1:9-11).

We are all familiar with this scene at the Jordan River, but we often overlook just how foundational it was to the rest of Jesus's ministry. Right at the beginning, before Jesus ever preached a sermon, before he ever healed the sick or fed the hungry, the Father gives him His blessing. From this point forward, Jesus knows who he is: he's God's Son. He knows His father loves him and is proud of him. Therefore, he doesn't need to spend a moment trying to prove his worthiness. He doesn't need the validation of the crowds; he's already got the validation of the One who truly matters.

This is exceptionally important, because do you remember the very next thing that happens after Jesus's baptism? He is led by the Spirit into the wilderness where he fasts for forty days. During this time, Satan comes and tries to derail Jesus's ministry before it even gets going.

The primary way that Satan tries to take Jesus out is through questioning his identity as the Father's Son. In Jesus's hunger, Satan tempts him to prove his identity - *"If you are the Son of God,* tell these stones to become bread" (Matthew 4:3 Emphasis added). Jesus dismisses his attempt. Next, the Tempter takes Jesus to the roof of the temple in Jerusalem and once again challenges his identity as the Son of God - *"If you truly are the Son of God,* then jump off, because scripture says that the angels won't even let you strike a heel against the stones below" (Matthew 4:6, my paraphrase). Once again, Jesus doesn't take the bait, because he is secure in his identity. He doesn't doubt what God has proclaimed over him for a moment, so he doesn't even give Satan's question a second thought.

Jesus had his Father's blessing, so he had no need to go looking for it from anyone else. He wasn't fretting about what other people thought of him. There was only one opinion that mattered to him – His Father's. Therefore, instead of having to pander to the crowds and worry about upsetting the power-brokers, he could spend his life carrying out his Father's business.

Struggling to Rest in God's Love

Admittedly, it is easy to dismiss Jesus's confidence in his relationship with the Father as unique. After all, he is God's only begotten son and he lived a perfect life. We are just a bunch of adopted kids who can't go a day without stumbling in sin one way or another. Even when we think we're doing well, pride is right there to trip us up. So it's easy for us to understand why God loves Jesus, but it's a lot harder to accept that He loves us, too.

Sure, the Bible tells us over and over that God loves us. He proved it by sending Jesus to die for us when we were still wallowing in our sin. But it is one thing to say, "God loves me," and yet another thing to truly rest in His love. We may get it intellectually, but often the truth of our Father's feelings about us has a hard time migrating from our head to our hearts.

I was a pastor for almost five years before I realized that I wasn't fully secure in the Father's love for me. It happened during an evening service while I was praying for a guy who had been struggling with feelings of inadequacy. As I was finishing my prayer over him, I felt the Spirit prompt me to bless him with the same blessing God had given Jesus at the Jordan River. So I told him, "I feel like God wants to tell you that He is your Father, who loves you and..." My prayer was left hanging in mid-sentence as I realized that I could not, in good conscience, tell this guy that God was pleased with him. In that moment, I honestly didn't know how God felt about him. So I wrapped up the prayer and moved on. However, throughout the rest of that evening I couldn't shake the unsettling feeling that I'd just stumbled into a major obstruction in my perception of God. I'd told countless people that our standing with the Father isn't dependent upon what we have done, but what Christ did for us. Yet here I was, wrestling with whether or not God was pleased with this guy and my first inclination was to question what he had done to earn God's pleasure.

That's when it hit me. I couldn't tell this guy he had the Father's full blessing, because I didn't believe that I had it either! I could accept that God loved me, but I just couldn't shake the belief that His pleasure was contingent upon my performance. This sent me into a considerable amount of soul searching. Over the next several months, I spent a lot of time praying, journaling and seeking out wise counsel to try and uncover why it was so hard for me to rest in the Father's love. And through this process, it slowly began to dawn on me that I was viewing God through the lens of my earthly father.

It's easy to do. After all, we call God our Father, so without realizing that we're doing it, we begin to view our Heavenly Father as a cosmic version of our earthly fathers. This, of course, can go sideways quickly. Our earthly dads are far from perfect. They carry within themselves the same fallen humanity that we do.

You may have had a dad who gave you his genes, but had no idea how to give you his blessing. The sad truth is that any guy can father a child, but not every guy knows how to be a father to his child. Few men ever take a class or read a book to help them grasp the awesome responsibility that they receive when they become a parent. Instead, they just wing it and hope for the best. Sadly, far too many fathers just end up passing on their destructive habits, coping mechanisms and insecurities to the next generation, just as Ted Turner's dad did for him. There really is something to the Biblical concept of the sins of the father being handed down to their children and their children's children.[51]

On the other hand, you may have had an exceptional father who went above and beyond the call of duty. Yet, even wonderful fathers cannot help but pass on some aspect of their fallen humanity. I was blessed with a dad who was a leader in our church and was highly regarded in our community. I never questioned whether he loved me, because he proved it through the countless ways he cared for my family. Yet, even in the midst of the stable, loving home that he and my mom provided, I still picked up the belief that my dad's approval was contingent upon my performance and that I fell woefully short of his expectations. Looking back, I can vividly remember a moment from my childhood that seemed to accentuate this point.

I was fourteen and our family was camping down in Mexico. I had been playing near the beach, but as I walked up toward the camp I was struck by the impulse to throw the football in my hand. I didn't stop to consider whether this was a good idea or who might catch it. I simply cocked my arm back and hurled the ball with all my might. Now, I've never been much of a quarterback. Most of my throws tend to wobble like a flat tire, but this one was a thing of beauty. I reveled in the tight spiral as the ball rose through the air and reached its apex. However, as it began to fall back toward terra firma at high velocity, I began to suspect that this might not have been the best idea. I couldn't control where the ball would land any more than I could undo the throw. As the ball sailed right into the middle of the camp, my cry of warning dug its heels into my throat and refused to come out. I winced as it landed right in the middle of the table where my dad was preparing dinner, splattering the front of his shirt in baked beans.

"EEEERRIC!"

My dad's voice cut through the otherwise calm evening and I suddenly felt like a convict walking to the gallows. As I crept into camp, my dad just stood there, covered in our dinner and shaking his head in exasperation. Then he said, "I'll be driving you to college," insinuating that with my impulsive nature I would never be responsible enough to be entrusted with a car.

Now, given the circumstances, his response was restrained to say the least. I wonder how I would have reacted if one of my boys had baptized me with baked beans. But the words struck home all the same, and they reaffirmed a subconscious belief that I carried around with me: "I'm a disappointment. I don't measure up to what my dad wants me to be." And so I did what so many others have done when faced with the displeasure of the person whose opinion means more to them than anyone else's – I set out to prove my worth.

Looking back over my adolescent years, so much of what I did was intended to show my dad that I was worthy of his approval. I tried my hardest at school, though I was never focused enough to get straight A's. I lettered all four years in water polo and swimming. I even resorted to reading thousand-page biographies about dead guys, because my dad had read them and I wanted to be able to talk with him about one of his interests. In all of these ways, and countless others, I sought to prove my worth to my dad, to prove that I was worthy of his respect. I wanted nothing more than to make him proud, but all too often it felt like I was a disappointment. And each time I messed up, each time I was reprimanded or grounded, was just another confirmation of my inadequacy.

When God Speaks with Our Father's Voice

Way too many of us live under a cloud of insecurity, a shadow cast by our earthly fathers. Whether they intended to or not, many of our fathers imparted to us the belief that we have to prove our worth or earn their love. So is it any wonder that when we draw near to our Heavenly Father, we feel the same need to prove our worth?

Stop and consider for a moment the ways your perception of God has been influenced by your earthly father. If your dad was demanding and critical, then it's likely that you will picture God with His arms crossed and a disappointed scowl on His face. If your dad was angry and abusive, then every time you encounter trouble in your life, you might chalk it up to God's punishment for one of your shortcomings. If your dad was absent from your life, then chances are you view God as distant and disinterested as well. Now, I'm not suggesting that God actually views and treats us like our dads did, but when we try to view Him through the lens of our earthly fathers, our perception will be distorted; it will be difficult for us to see our Heavenly Father for who He truly is. Let me to give you an example.

I have a friend whose father was verbally abusive to him as he was growing up. The man would regularly call his son names like "idiot" and "stupid." And his words penetrated my buddy's tough outer shell and took root in his heart. Recently, I was talking with my friend about an area of sin that he continually finds himself struggling to overcome, and I asked him what He thinks God would say to him in the midst of his struggles. Almost without thinking, my friend blurted, "I think he'd tell me, 'Quit being such an idiot and cut it out!'" I was surprised by the harshness of my friend's tone and I couldn't help but note that this didn't sound much like God's voice at all. It sounded a lot like his dad's.

Far too many of us have learned to hear the Father's voice through the corrupted filter of our own dad's voice. We've internalized things our dads spoke over us, their criticisms or angry outbursts, and then we stamp God's name over those mental recordings as if He's the one who said them. Without thinking about it, we conclude that God looks at us in the same way our dads did, and then we begin to interact with our Heavenly Father in the same way we interacted with our earthly one. If we were resentful and rebellious with our dads, then chances are we'll resent God's overbearing nature and find ourselves automatically rebelling against Him as well. If we sought to win our dad's approval, then we'll find ourselves performing for God's approval as well. Despite what the Bible might tell us about how our Father in Heaven feels about us, our perceptions of Him will be naturally influenced by the men that raised us - or at least should have.

A New Perspective on the Father's Love

Looking back on my own spiritual journey, I can see how my view of God was influenced by my relationship with my dad. I never questioned my dad's love for me, but I was under the impression that I had to prove myself in order to make him proud of me. Therefore, despite the Bible's affirmation that God's love for us isn't based upon our effort or worthiness, I couldn't shake the belief that His love for me was tied to my performance.

However, my skewed perception of God's love was forever changed on the day that I became a father myself. For the first time in my life, I got a glimpse of what unconditional love actually looks like, and it began to help me understand just how deeply my Heavenly Father loves me. When my firstborn, Ethan, was a baby, all he could do was eat, sleep and soil his diapers, but I loved that kid more than I'd ever loved anything else in the world. There was nothing he could do to make me stop loving him, because there was nothing he'd done to earn my love. He was my boy, period!

He's older now and, like me, he can act impulsively. Sometimes stuff accidentally gets broken or people get hurt. When that happens, I have to discipline him; I'm responsible to God for training him up into the man that God has created him to be. However, that doesn't mean that my love for him ever wavers. He is my boy. He will always be my boy and I make sure he knows that.

When he's sitting in time out, often with tears in his eyes, I like to sit down next to him and tell him: "Ethan, I love you so much. Why do you think that is?" He will smile through the tears and answer, "Because I'm your boy." Then I'll remind him, "Ethan, it doesn't matter what you do, I will never stop loving you. You are my son and I'm so grateful God has entrusted you to your mom and me."

I don't ever want my sons to wonder how their daddy feels about them. I don't want them to buy into the belief that they have to earn my love or prove their worth in order to be accepted by me or by their Heavenly Father.

Now, if I, a sinful and selfish man, can love my boys so deeply and so unconditionally, imagine how much more deeply and unconditionally our Heavenly Father loves us. He loves us so much that He died for us! And His sacrifice wasn't motivated by any effort on our part. It's not like we had been trying to live righteously and He decided to help us out a little. No, He moved toward us when we were still dead set on going our own way and doing our own thing; as Paul wrote in his letter to the Romans, "God demonstrates His own love for us in this: While we were still sinners, Christ died for us" (Romans 5:8). That's how much our Father in Heaven loves us.

Jesus told a parable to illustrate the all-consuming, never-wavering love that the Father has for us. There was a young boy who had grown tired of waiting for his dad to die so that he could get his hands on his inheritance. This boy goes to his father and asks him for what he has coming. This request is tantamount to him saying, "Dad, I wish you were dead, because I want my inheritance now." Now, the father in the story has every right to disown his son on the spot for the offensiveness of his request, but he doesn't. Instead, this father, who represents our Heavenly Father in the story, gives in to his son's request. He liquidates some of his estate and gives it to the boy, who then goes off to a distant place and starts to live it up. The kid throws lavish parties surrounded by an entourage of fair-weather friends, who love him while the money is flowing. Yet, as soon as his funds run out, his so-called friends quickly follow suit.

All of a sudden, the kid finds himself wallowing in a pig-sty, covered in the muck of his mistakes. His belly rumbles and, though he has become used to caviar and filet mignon, he is tempted to fill his stomach with the slop he has been feeding the pigs. As he sits there, wallowing in the filth of his short-sighted choices, he begins to think about home and how well he had it there. Even the servants in his father's household live better than he is living now. A thought begins to germinate in his mind: "Maybe the man I used to call dad will take me back. Not as his son. That's asking for too much. But perhaps he will allow me to be a servant in the house I used to call my home." So, with that desperate hope in mind, he begins the long, shame-filled trek home to beg the mercy of the man he used to call "dad."

Jesus's story suddenly shifts perspective from the son to the father, who has been waiting at home, holding out hope that his prodigal son would one day return. As he stands on his porch, scanning the horizon, the father sees a solitary figure come into view, head hung low and shoulders sagging.

"Can it be? Is it him?"

Suddenly, the father recognizes his boy and he springs into action. Now, given how disrespectfully the son had treated him, we might expect this father to stand on the porch with his arms crossed, waiting for the kid to finish his walk of shame before unloading his wrath on the boy. But this father, who represents our Heavenly Father, does something far more unexpected. He hitches up his robes in a most undignified manner and begins sprinting down the walkway toward his wayward son. And when he reaches him, he doesn't stand far off and lay into his boy for the mistakes he has made. He doesn't even give his son time to say his "I blew it" speech that he had no doubt been rehearsing over those long, lonesome miles. Instead, the father throws his arms around his boy and welcomes him home with kisses.

The son is understandably taken aback. This isn't the sort of homecoming he had expected, and he awkwardly starts into his prepared speech: "Father, I messed up and I don't deserve to be called your son." Yet, his dad dismisses the idea that he would ever disown his child. Instead, he sends some servants to fetch a new, clean robe and a ring for his boy's finger, and he tells them to prepare a party. "For this son of mine was dead and is alive again; he was lost and is found" (Luke 15:24). And so the celebration begins.

That's how God feels toward you, whether you can accept it or not. When we stop trying to earn our righteousness and simply rest in the gift of grace that Jesus bought for us on the cross, God welcomes us home with open arms and a celestial party. He recognizes that we are each prodigals at heart, prone to run, but He never stops loving us or longing for reconciliation. Even after our conversion, as we stumble toward holiness through the enablement of His Spirit, our Father doesn't fixate on our mistakes. He doesn't sit back with arms crossed and a disappointed look on His face as if He's sorry He ever adopted us in the first place. No, He looks at us with an unwavering love that only a parent can truly understand. Sure, our choices may grieve His heart. After all, He knows how our sins can hurt both ourselves and those around us. But He doesn't ever stop loving us, not even for a moment.

So you can stop trying to earn the Father's love; you already have it! There's nothing you can do to make Him love you more, and there's nothing you can do to make Him love you less. You are His child, redeemed by the blood of Jesus, and just watching you grow into the man or woman that He's made you to be brings him pleasure.

May you stop striving to prove your worth and simply rest in the love that your Father has for you. May you rest securely in your identity as His beloved son or daughter, so that you don't need your spouse or your kids or your job or your peers or anything else to tell you that you are acceptable. May you stop running from your mistakes and stop trying to make up for them, since Jesus already died to do that. Instead, may you run with reckless abandon into the arms of your Father in Heaven, who loves you more than you could ever possibly fathom.

I echo Paul's prayer, "that you, being rooted and established in love, may have power, together with all the Lord's holy people, to grasp how wide and long and high and deep is the love of Christ, and to know this love that surpasses knowledge—that you may be filled to the measure of all the fullness of God" (Ephesians 3:17-19).

Think About It -

- What was your relationship with your own father like?

- How has your relationship with your earthly father influenced the way you view and approach your Heavenly Father?

- Jesus was secure in the face of opposition and public criticism because he already had his Father's blessing. Did your father ever bestow his blessing upon you? How has your life been affected by the presence or absence of your father's blessing?

- How might your life be different if you could rest in the Father's unwavering love for you?

CHAPTER 11

Green Pastures and Dark Valleys

I don't know what the future holds, but I do know who holds my future.
– Ralph Abernathy

One of the most common questions I get as a pastor is, "If God loves us, then why does He allow us to suffer so much?" It's a fair question. But it exposes an underlying assumption that many of us carry within us without even realizing it: we figure that God's love should naturally result in our comfort and safety.

It's easy to see how we come to this conclusion. After all, when a child is born, parents do everything they can to remove every discomfort. Each time my wife and I brought one of our sons home from the hospital, we would feed him on demand, change his dirty diapers, and comfort him whenever he would start to cry. But as my boys grew, our approach to parenting shifted from coddling to training. At first, we helped them learn how to get through a night without having to be fed every three hours. Then we taught them how to fall asleep on their own, without being rocked incessantly. Later on, we helped them learn how to listen to their bodies and use the toilet rather than a diaper.

Each of these transitions was an important step in their growth process, but that doesn't mean that my boys liked it. Whenever we hit one of those transitional milestones and their mom and I set out to teach them how to do something on their own, they'd throw a wall-eyed fit.

When we were trying to potty-train my youngest son, Grayson, he would often run off and hide so that he could soil in his diaper in peace. He had no desire to sit on that cold, white seat to do his business. When the smell finally led us to where he was hiding, he would invariably throw a tantrum when we tried to change him. I'll admit that at times I was tempted to ignore the issue so that we wouldn't have to weather another emotional storm. Sometimes I just wanted to say, "You want to sit in your mess? Fine by me! Just go down wind." But what kind of parent would I be if I never potty-trained my boy? I don't even want to think about the torment he'd endure if he showed up to grade school in a diaper.

So we braved the emotional outbursts and slowly trained our sons. It wasn't particularly easy, but in the long run it was well worth it. Similarly, our Father in Heaven cares more about our character than He does our momentary comfort, so He, too, allows us to undergo seasons of intense discomfort.

Following My Shepherd

I vividly recall a painful season of spiritual growth that I walked through a few years back. I was a new father, an adjunct professor at a local Christian college and an associate pastor at a rapidly growing church. Life was exciting and I was running hard and fast. It felt like there were never enough hours in the day to do everything I needed to get done, and my relationships with my family and with God bore the brunt of my harried schedule. Whenever my wife would ask me to choose her and our infant son over work, I would feel frustrated. Couldn't she see that everything I was doing was for them?! Wasn't it enough that I was providing for them and serving God? Speaking of God, during this season I was acting a lot like Martha. I was far too busy working for God to actually spend any time with Him. So I drove myself into exhaustion, never realizing that I was in danger of burning out. Looking back, I can clearly see the warning signs. I was red-lining and running on fumes, but the excitement of feeling needed kept me going. Little did I know that a breakdown was imminent.

It's funny how people around us can see the warning signs better than we can. I was physically present, but emotionally distant. My marriage was suffering and my desire to minister to others was waning. It was even hard to scrape together the desire to worship at church. A couple times, I chose to read in my office rather than sit through another service. Something was amiss; I was in a funk and everyone around me could tell. So one day, my boss pulled me into his office and voiced his concern. "Eric, I don't know what's going on with you, but the joy-filled guy that I know is gone," he told me. "I'm concerned about you and I want you to take a few days off to spend some time with God and your wife." Now, I know that he only wanted the best for me, but in the moment it felt like I'd been called into the principal's office and suspended.

I went home and collapsed into the couch with my wife, feeling utterly defeated. Thankfully, it was my son's nap time and we spent the next couple hours praying together for God's wisdom and direction. During that time, I saw a mental picture of myself lying in a bed, covered up to my neck in a bed-sheet; in the vision, the sheet was pulled away and my body was withered and emaciated. I knew in my heart that God was showing me the state of my spirit, which had grown dry from pouring out without ever stopping to be refilled. It feels ironic to admit that, as a pastor, I had grown spiritually dry, but it was true. In my drive to care for others' needs, I had neglected my own relationship with God. I was pouring into other people out of the dregs, not the overflow of my heart. Ministry had become an obligation, not a joy and, although I didn't realize it in that moment, my Father in Heaven was putting me on the sideline for my own good and the good of those who depended upon me the most.

Over the next few days, God drew me toward one passage in particular, a familiar Psalm that took on far greater significance as

my journey continued. During a time of quiet reflection during my
forced sabbatical, God led me to Psalm 23. David's words felt as if
they were written specifically for me in that moment:

> The LORD is my shepherd; I shall not be in want.
>> He makes me lie down in green pastures,
> he leads me beside quiet waters,
>> he restores my soul.
> He guides me along paths of righteousness
>> for his name's sake.
> Even though I walk
>> through the valley of the shadow of death,
> I will fear no evil,
>> for you are with me;
> your rod and your staff,
>> they comfort me.
> You prepare a table before me
>> in the presence of my enemies.
> You anoint my head with oil;
>> my cup overflows.
> Surely goodness and love will follow me
>> all the days of my life,
> and I will dwell in the house of the LORD
>> forever.

In the coming months, every single verse of this beautiful,
ancient cry of dependence and trust would come to have a special
significance to me, but on that particular morning, it was the first
four lines that spoke most powerfully to me:

> The LORD is my shepherd, I shall not be in want.
>> He makes me lie down in green pastures,
> he leads me beside quiet waters,
>> he restores my soul.

As I sat in the early morning stillness of my home, alone with God as everyone else in the house was still asleep, I felt as if my Shepherd was telling me that He needed to pull me out of ministry so that He could minister to me. He warned me that He was going to make me lie down in a green pasture and rest, which was going to be painful for someone like me who was currently finding his identity and validation through what I did. However, the purpose of this time was not going to be punitive, but rather healing. He was going to restore my soul.

And so God invited me into a season of spiritual renewal. It was a scary invitation, because it would require me to let go of everything that I'd built my identity upon. It would also require my wife and me to trust God in every way: financially, emotionally, spiritually and physically. But who better to trust than the Creator and Sustainer of life, the only One who brings the dead back to life?! So we accepted the invitation and when I returned to work a couple days later, it was to clean out my desk rather than to resume my duties as a pastor.

I'd love to tell you that I made this choice with confidence and joy, but I'd be lying. I did it with a ton of fear and anxiety. After all, I was the primary bread winner for my family and I had a young wife and son at home. I remember thinking, "God, are you going to take care of us?" But no sooner did the question cross my mind than His Spirit within remind me, "The LORD is my shepherd, I shall not be in want." I felt a lot like one of the Israelites walking out of bondage in Egypt, following God into the wilderness. I didn't know what the future held, but I knew who held my future and I chose to trust Him in spite of my fears.

I'd also love to tell you that the next eight months were easy and exhilarating, but, again, I'd be lying. Though there were certainly moments of excitement and joy, it was a season marked more by pain than anything else. I'm not talking physical pain, but rather the pain of having to watch my false-self die. After all, in order to bring me to the point where I could rest in Him, my Father first had to show me the insufficiency of trusting in my own strength. He intentionally led me away from the work that I'd used to define myself so that I'd realize that I was not the sum total of what I did. And He specifically told me that I wasn't allowed to try and shorten this season of soul-restoration by looking for work; He simply wanted me to rest in Him.

While I was in the midst of that season, it felt like I was walking through the Valley of the Shadow of Death, and I couldn't help but think that the only reason He would lead me through the valley was because He was guiding me to toward a nicer, greener, more comfortable pasture on the other side. But God challenged this mindset one morning during a time of prayer and journaling. The following is an excerpt from that journal entry:

> *What if this broken road isn't intended to lead me to a greener pasture? What if the purpose of this path is to draw me into a deeper, more intimate relationship with my shepherd? Through this whole journey, I've held onto the belief that God has called me out of a comfortable place in order to prepare me for something better. And so I've followed Him with confidence that the more painful the journey, the greater the payoff in the end. And this whole time I've interpreted "payoff" to mean a better, more comfortable place to rest on the other side of this valley. Yet, comfort probably isn't God's ultimate intention. From everything I've read about Him in scripture, those He called to follow Him weren't usually rewarded with lucrative, comfortable positions in life. In fact, most of them continued to suffer, sacrificing jobs, family support, health, even their lives in the pursuit of their Lord. So I need to ask the question: "If the only fruit that this season produces is a more intimate relationship with my Lord, one where I learn to trust His lead and His pace no matter how counter-cultural it may be, am*

*I willing to follow Him regardless of the cost?" While I
don't like the thought, the only answer I can give is "Of
course. Where else would I go? He is the only source of
life and true purpose." So lead on, Jesus. My family will
follow. Wherever you want to take us and whatever pace
you want to set is your prerogative. We choose to trust
you. Just, please be gentle.*

Green Pastures

As I mentioned, this season felt like walking through the Valley
of the Shadow of Death. But as I look back on that time, I've come
to realize that I wasn't actually in a valley at all. In hindsight, I've
come to see that He was actually forcing me to lie down in a green
pasture. Though it felt like I was dying, that was only my false sense
of self-sufficiency crying out as God made me stop striving so that
I could rest in Him.

When we think about green pastures, our western minds tend
to pull up a picture of vibrant green, rolling hills under a beautiful
blue sky. These are the green pastures of the American heartland,
but we have to remember that David, the writer of this Psalm,
was a shepherd in Israel where the grazing lands are radically
different. I've seen the land that Israeli shepherds bring the sheep
to graze upon and it's anything but lush and green. What they
refer to as green pastures are actually rocky hillsides with a few
tufts of wild grass growing here and there. This is an important
distinction, because when we think of God making us lie down in
green pastures, we naturally envision a field where the ground is
cushy, the grass is plentiful and everything we could possibly need
is within arm's reach. This sort of mental image gives the false
impression that it should be easy and comfortable to rest in a green
pasture. Quite often, it's not.

Have you ever considered how ironic it is that the Good
Shepherd would have to "make" us lie down in green pastures? I

sure have. If it's comfortable, the sheep probably aren't going to fight it. But the green pastures that David is referring to is land that you and I would probably consider to be more like the wilderness than a pasture. It's not the sort of place where we can just take our eyes off of the shepherd and rest in comfort. Rather, our comfort comes from the proximity of our shepherd. He is the one that leads us to the grazing grounds. He is the one who leads us beside still waters where we can be refreshed. He's the one who guides us along paths of righteousness and He does so "for His name's sake," not for our own. It's so easy to forget that we are sheep and, when we do, we tend to take our eyes off the shepherd and rely on our own strength.

I'll confess that one of the primary reasons that eight-month season of soul restoration was so uncomfortable was that my Shepherd made me lie down and forced me to stop trying to provide for myself. He made me rest in His provision, and I don't like to feel totally dependent. Sure, I'd love to see God provide like He did for the Israelites in the wilderness, waking up each morning to a fresh layer of manna on the ground, but I don't actually want to be dependent upon that provision. I want to know that I've got a few granola bars stashed in the tent just in case there's no manna that morning. Dependence is difficult to embrace, but that's precisely what the Shepherd of my Soul was trying to teach me: stop striving, stop trying to prove your worth. Just rest in my care, because I love you, and my love is enough.

I wish I had the space to tell you all the ways that God proved Himself to be a faithful, trustworthy Shepherd through that season. I'll just hit a couple of the highlights: He provided for our needs in ways that I still can't explain. Cashier's checks showed up in our mailbox out of the blue and our bank account never seemed to fluctuate even though I'd walked away from our primary source of income. Even more remarkable was the impact this season of restoration had on my relationship with both my wife and with my God.

Prior to this journey into the green pasture, my marriage was strained to the breaking point. It seemed to me that everyone in the world appreciated what I was doing except for my wife, the one person who I felt should have been most supportive. All she seemed to want me to do was slow down and I resented her for suggesting it.

A funny thing about relationships – there are things we like and things we dislike about people and, like two sides of the same coin, we are usually only able to see one side at a time. In the early stages of a relationship, we tend to only look at the positives, but given enough time, the coin will get flipped and we will start to fixate on the flaws. Before God led me into that green pasture, I was fixated on my wife's flaws, constantly picking her apart in my mind and verbally venting my displeasure far too often. Yet, no sooner did God make me lie down and rest then He flipped the coin over and reminded me of the myriad reasons why I fell in love with my wife in the first place. He began to rekindle my appreciation for the woman that He had entrusted to my care. In a time when I was intimately familiar with my weakness, I realized just how strong she really was. Several times during those months, I found myself weeping with gratitude for the gift God had given me in my wife. Needless to say, our relationship flourished in the green pasture.

The other relationship that was radically altered was my relationship with God Himself. Now that I was no longer running around like a chicken with my head cut off, all in the name of serving God, I suddenly realized just how much I longed to be near Him. Like a castaway that has been adrift over a sea of salt-water, I'd forgotten how thirsty I was until I got that first sip of fresh, life-restoring water, and then all I wanted was more. So, like Martha's sister, Mary, I simply sat in God's presence and allowed Him to replenish my soul. I drank deeply of His presence, spending hours in prayer and journaling. I couldn't get enough of His Word. I was surprised to find that once I stopped studying the Bible in order to find teaching points and just read, it suddenly started speaking directly to me and nourishing my soul.

One of the greatest temptations for a minister is to entertain the belief that we graduate from being one of the sheep when we become a shepherd. We begin to think that we can serve God without resting in Him and allowing Him to direct our steps. But regardless of our position and calling in life, we are all, first and foremost, sheep under our Shepherd's capable watch. The more we can allow ourselves to rest in His care, the better it will go for both ourselves and everyone around us.

In short, just because we feel uncomfortable doesn't mean God has got us in a dark valley. He may actually have us in a green pasture where He is forcing us to stop and rest so that He can restore our soul.

Of course, this doesn't mean that He will never lead us through dark valleys.

Walking Through Dark Valleys

It's tempting to buy into the belief that if we truly love our Shepherd and are following His lead, then we will never experience any true pain. Sadly, this just isn't the case. Plenty of faithful men and women in the Bible suffered greatly in spite of their faithfulness, sometimes even because of it. John the Baptist was beheaded. Stephen, the first Christian martyr, was stoned to death for proclaiming the gospel. Peter was crucified upside down during Nero's persecution of the Christians. Paul endured beatings, stoning, imprisonment, and persecution. The poor guy was shipwrecked not once, but three times.[52] And in the end, he died for his faith. If that isn't enough evidence, every Easter we remember the fact that our Lord and Savior, Jesus Christ, was beaten and ultimately killed for us.

No, following Jesus does not guarantee us easy, comfortable lives. In fact, Jesus himself warned us that "in this world you will have trouble" (John 16:33). This isn't simply because we sin, though we can definitely bring suffering upon ourselves because of our choices. Sometimes we suffer because of other people's choices.

I think of all the children who have had to weather a divorce or grow up in a broken home. They did nothing to bring this suffering upon themselves, but that doesn't mean they're immune to the consequences. And sometimes we experience hardship simply because we live in a fallen, corrupted world. [53]

If there's one thing we can count on in life, it's that we will walk through some dark valleys – through seasons of pain and suffering. This pain can take a lot of forms: we may have our hearts broken by people we trusted, our bodies might be racked by sickness or disease, people we love might die, we may have to live under an oppressive cloud of anxiety or depression, or we may have to contend with a chronic addiction. There's no end to the types of hardship we may have to face throughout our lives. I don't write this to discourage you, but rather to acknowledge the harsh reality of life in a fallen world. In this world we will have trouble.

However, Jesus wasn't simply making some fatalistic declaration that life would be hard and then we die. Though it's true that we will each face hardship, that's not the point he was driving at. Jesus told his disciples, "In this world you will have trouble. But take heart! I have overcome the world" (John 16:33). In other words, in this world you will suffer, but be encouraged by the fact that your suffering will not get the last word! Because of what Jesus did on the cross, dying to break sin's grip and make a way for prodigals like us to come home, we can find hope in the midst of the suffering. We can find peace in the midst of the tears and the unknowns. Though the trials we face might seem overwhelming, we can rest in the knowledge that God is bigger than our troubles, He's bigger than our pain, and He can bring beauty from the ashes of our lives.

I wish I could talk about the dark valley as a generality, as something that affects people out there but of which I have no personal experience. In truth, I've walked through my fair share of dark valleys, none darker than the premature birth of my second son, Grayson.

On August 24, 2011, my wife was twenty-seven weeks pregnant

and everything was looking good. Sure we had our concerns; what expecting parent doesn't? But we'd bathed our unborn son in prayer and, since I was a pastor, I figured God would make sure everything went smoothly. However, as we sat on the couch watching television, the unthinkable happened: my wife's water broke thirteen weeks prematurely and we were unexpectedly, violently thrust into a dark valley. I remember that night so vividly: the fear in my wife's eyes as the truth of what was happening dawned on her, the long drive along empty freeways as we raced to the hospital; the swarm of nurses who buzzed around my terrified bride, trying to get her contractions to stop so that they could transport her to another hospital that was better equipped to care for a severely premature baby. And over all of this was an overwhelming sense of powerlessness; I could do absolutely nothing to fix this. All I could do was stand beside my girl and endure it with her.

The nurses were able to get my wife stabilized, and for about a week and a half we were able to keep the little guy inside his mom, buying him precious days to grow. But on September 4, 2011, the doctors discovered that he had stopped moving in the womb and they feared the worst, so they wheeled my wife into an unscheduled C-Section before the damage was irreparable.

Grayson was unceremoniously dragged into the world eleven weeks before his due date and things were touch and go from the start. Over the next 48 hours, things went from bad to worse. It turned out he had an infection, which had traveled into his spinal fluid, so he was put on a heavy dose of antibiotics. Furthermore, his lungs collapsed not once, but twice. As if that wasn't enough, the doctors warned us that there might be bleeding in his brain, which could cause permanent brain damage. I can't think of another time in my life when I felt so utterly powerless. I so desperately wanted to pick my boy up to comfort him, to let him know that he wasn't alone in this cold, sterile world, but he was so fully covered in tubes and wires that I couldn't even lift his little 3 pound body. Did I mention I felt powerless?!

There, in the depths of that dark valley, I couldn't help but wonder, "Why, God? Why would you allow this to happen? What have I done wrong? What did we do to deserve this?" My questions exposed my assumption that what we were going through was a natural repercussion for some mistake my wife or I had made, that God was nothing more than a cosmic vending machine that dispenses blessings when we do good, but curses when we mess up. At the time, I couldn't understand that what we were enduring was simply the result of life in a fallen world. To be honest, I couldn't see much as my wife and I limped through that dark valley that we found ourselves in. All we could do was cling to one another and take each day as it came.

Yet, as we emerged from the depths of the valley and got some perspective on the broken path God was leading us down, I began to recognize the way our Shepherd was right there in the midst of the valley with us, guiding us step by step, giving us the courage and the strength to stumble through each day and each challenge. Once again, I will share a brief except from my journal that I wrote about a month and a half after my son's birth, because it illustrates the sweet fruit that can grow in the midst of even the darkest valleys.

> *As I survey the broken path that our family has limped down, what looked so dark and foreboding heading in takes on an unexpected sweetness in hindsight. I think of the doctors and nurses that have become more than attendants – they've become friends and prayer warriors along with us. I think of our family and friends who have supported us all along the way, helped us shoulder our emotional and physical burdens, and lifted up our son and our family in prayer throughout. I think of the way I celebrate what we had taken for granted with our firstborn: that Grayson can breathe on his own; that his ears and eyes are developing normally; that he can*

drink milk; that he continues to grow gram by gram, ounce by ounce. And I think of the way Grayson's story and God's faithfulness in the midst of the complications has reminded me (and others) that the goal of life isn't becoming more comfortable and safe.

I've become increasingly convinced that the purpose of life is to grow ever more intimately familiar with my Creator; to learn how to walk with Him and to live a life that reflects His heart and His love to a world that would rather deny His existence. Though I wouldn't have chosen the path we've taken over these last couple months, I can't help but admit that it has drawn me much deeper into the arms of my Father God. I've learned to see the beauty in the broken path we've journeyed down. As I look into my son's deep blue eyes which are processing light months before they were designed to, as I hold his tiny hands and watch his chest rise and fall in spite of the abuse his lungs have taken, I see a gift from God that goes beyond the birth of my second son. I see a growing, breathing testimony to God's grace. I see a living reminder that what the world holds up as God's blessing is often nothing more than the easy, comfortable path that allows us to be self-reliant.

No, my son's entrance into the world may not have been what we expected, but God has been with us through every step of the way. So I thank God for the broken path He has allowed us to travel down, because it has forced us to lean into Him rather than simply resting in our own strength.

Dark valleys are painful, but that doesn't mean that they can't be redemptive as well. Often, it's in the midst of the valley that we realize just how good our God truly is and just how much He loves us. There's a cliché that's thrown around in Christian circles:

"God won't give you more than you can handle." It sounds good in theory, but it's a promise found nowhere in scripture.[54] And I can personally attest that when it came to Grayson's birth, God gave us way more than we could handle on our own. I can also point to plenty of others who are currently wrestling with something far greater than they can handle by their own strength – sickness, addiction, depression, anxiety. However, the good news of the Bible is that we're not alone, that our hope isn't in our own strength, but in our God. So while God may give us more than we can handle, He never gives us more than He can handle.

One redemptive gift of the dark valleys is the reminder that we are not alone, that we have a Shepherd who loves us and is there to guide our steps and care for our needs. But He cares more about our character than our comfort, so He's not averse to leading us along broken paths that strengthen and refine us. As Jesus warned us, in this world we will have trouble, but we can take heart that our God has overcome the pain of this world. So although we may suffer and stumble along these broken paths, we have hope that even the deepest, darkest valleys won't get the last word and that what the world calls a curse, God can use to accomplish His purposes in and through us.

The Father's Training

Suffering may be a natural part of life in this sin-scarred world, but that doesn't mean that it is meaningless and serves no purpose. Our God has an amazing ability to redeem even the most painful trials we walk through; He can use our hardship to train us up.

The author of Hebrews exhorts us to "endure hardship as discipline; God is treating you as his children. For what children are not disciplined by their father?" (Hebrews 12:7). Don't get caught up on that word discipline. We tend to equate discipline with punishment, but that's not what this verse is getting at. Rather, it's focusing on the way that a father trains up or instructs his children so that they will grow in maturity. Discipline is the means by which a child is taught to grow in responsibility. It's a primary tool that a father uses to refine his children's character. In the case of our Heavenly Father, hardship is the primary tool that He uses to strengthen and refine us.

The writer of Hebrews goes on to explain that "no discipline seems pleasant at the time, but painful. Later on, however, it produces a harvest of righteousness and peace for those who have been trained by it" (Hebrews 12: 11). Regardless of whether our suffering is brought on by our own sinful choices, the sinful choices of someone else, or is just a product of living in a broken world, the fact is we have a God who can redeem our suffering and use it to mature us. Whether we find ourselves resting in a green pasture or stumbling through a dark valley, our Father can use our circumstances to strengthen our character and increase our faith in Him. Of course, if we hope to receive this "harvest of righteousness and peace," we actually need to allow our Shepherd to train us through those trying times.

When we face adversity, we have a choice in how we respond. We could get angry and resentful toward God and anyone else that we can blame. We could throw up our hands and cry, "It's not fair! I don't deserve this." But if we take that approach, we probably won't learn anything valuable through our trial. We will take nothing from it but the personal confirmation that we are a victim in the cosmic game of life. On the other hand, we can choose to place our trust in God and lean into our hardship. We can rely on His Spirit within us for the strength to persevere and the wisdom to know how to respond. And if we do, then we will grow, we will mature, and we will come to recognize that our Father truly is trustworthy.

Personal growth isn't the only fruit that can be produced in the soil of suffering. Our attitude in the midst of our trials speaks volumes about what we truly believe. Talk is cheap. It's easy to say we trust God when the sun is shining and the path is level. But when the storm clouds gather and we find ourselves stumbling through a dark valley, suddenly our words carry more weight. It's in the midst of suffering that our true beliefs are exposed. So if we are willing to fix our eyes on our Shepherd and follow His lead, God can use us in the midst of our trials to be a beacon of hope to a skeptical and hurting world.

I don't know what you are going through or what you will go through, but I do know that just because you experience suffering and hardship in your life doesn't mean that God has turned His back on you. Similarly, the presence of pain in your life does not necessarily mean that you are outside of your Father's will. Regardless of whether He wants you to walk down this broken path or He is simply allowing it to happen, this one thing we can be certain of: God can redeem it. He can use it to bring about His purposes in your life and in the lives of others around you.

Because of this, Paul declares that we should "rejoice in our sufferings, because we know that suffering produces perseverance; perseverance, character; and character, hope" (Romans 5:3-4). Now, he's not suggesting that we should rejoice that we are suffering. Rather, he calls us to rejoice in the midst of our suffering, in the midst of the green pastures and the dark valleys. Why? Because, by God's grace and guidance, our suffering will not be for nothing and it won't get the last word.

I think of two of my friends who are currently undergoing cancer treatment. Paul isn't suggesting that they be grateful that they have cancer, but he is suggesting that they rejoice in the midst of their cancer. He would encourage them to rejoice that they aren't overcome by their affliction, that our God is bigger than their disease, and that He can use it for good. That's not to say that they won't experience pain as they journey down this broken path. Nor does it mean that they are guaranteed that the cancer will go into remission. However, because of the hope they have in Christ, it does mean that regardless of what happens, their cancer will not get the last word. Whether in this life or in the life to come, they will be healed completely; they will be cancer free and pain free.

Therefore we do not lose heart. Though outwardly we are wasting away, yet inwardly we are being renewed day by day. For our light and momentary troubles are achieving for us an eternal glory that far outweighs them all. So we fix our eyes not on what is seen, but on what is unseen, since what is seen is temporary, but what is unseen is eternal. (2 Corinthians 4:16-18)

Think About It –

- Read Psalm 23. Which parts stand out to you? Why?

- In what ways have you found God to be a good shepherd?

- Describe a time that He made you lie down in a green pasture?

- What did He teach you through that time?

- Describe a dark valley that God has led you through?

- What did He teach you through that time?

CHAPTER 12

Ambassadors of Hope

Here at last is the thing I was made for.
- CS Lewis

As we have seen in previous chapters, God created mankind for
a unique purpose: to be His representatives. He made us in His
image so that we could be stewards over His creation. Sadly, this
arrangement didn't last long. As soon as Satan planted the idea
that God wasn't being fully trustworthy, that He was holding out
on Adam and Eve, they took matters into their own hands, eating
the very fruit that their Creator commanded them to avoid. In
that moment, sin entered the world and began to wreak havoc.
It warped the first man and woman's perception of themselves
and sent them into hiding, both from God and one another. On
top of that, it severed the intimate connection they had with their
Creator and enslaved them. This was perhaps the darkest chapter
of human history, and the effects of that one decision are still felt
today. Thankfully God didn't give up on humanity.

Though sin created a chasm that separated mankind from our
God, He wasn't willing to simply turn His back on us. In spite of
sin's corruption, His love for us never wavered and He made a way
for us to be reconciled to Him: God sent His son, Jesus Christ, to
take on human flesh and die in our place. He didn't do this because

we had earned it. He did it because of His love for us, an unwavering love that isn't based upon our performance. So, because of the cross, we who were formerly slaves to sin have become adopted sons and daughters of the King. We prodigals who have run so far from home can finally return and rest in our Father's love. And when we turn our hearts toward home and place our faith in Him, He places His Spirit within us as a mark of His ownership as well as the means by which He helps us better reflect His image.

That's the gospel message, the good news of Jesus Christ. But it's incomplete. There is still one final aspect of God's redemptive gift of grace that we have yet to explore - not only has Christ's sacrifice restored our relationship with our Father, it's restored the very purpose for which God created us: to be His representatives to a hurting world.

So, let's go back to a familiar place where we started our journey together. Let's go back to the graveyard where Jesus was confronted by a raving lunatic and see the way that He breathed new life and new purpose into a man that the world had given up on.

A Return to the Graveyard

"What is your name?"

Jesus' question hung in the air and the gathered disciples watched the madman warily, waiting for his reply. For a time, the disheveled man from the tombs seemed like he wouldn't respond at all, but then he finally spoke.

"I am Legion," he answered, "because of the number of demons inside."

Several of the disciples standing closest to the demon-possessed man anxiously took a step back, but the man who called himself Legion simply remained where he was, his wild eyes locked on Jesus. Then he spoke again.

"I know who you are and I know the authority you have. Please don't force us from this area." Jesus just returned the man's gaze, watching and considering his response.

"I beg you, Son of God, don't cast us from here," the madman implored. Still Jesus watched him silently. The man's unease grew more palpable and he began to glance around, hoping to find support from the disciples, but he saw only a mixture of fear and curiosity on their faces. Finally, his eyes rested upon the herd of pigs rooting along the rocky hillside nearby. "The pigs! Send us into the pigs, and we will leave this man alone."

Jesus simply nodded, giving his ascent, and the man's body was thrown violently to the ground and began writhing in the dust. Then, as quickly as it had started, his thrashing stopped and his body went deathly still. A couple of the disciples leaned in closer, trying to determine whether the man was even breathing.

Suddenly, a frantic squeal rose up from the hillside nearby. It quickly grew to a chorus of squeals as the demons entered the pigs. In a matter of moments, the whole herd was thrown into a frenzy, and they began to race up the hillside like a frightened school of fish trying to escape an unseen predator. The hill ended abruptly in a sheer cliff, dropping away to the sea below. In their agitated state, the herd either didn't see the danger or didn't care, because pig after pig raced right over the edge and plummeted to the sea below.

The men who had been tending the herd were left standing with mouths agape, their surprise giving way to dread as the last of the thrashing pigs drowned in the lake. Someone would have to answer for this financial disaster. They glanced over toward Jesus and his disciples, looking for answers, then turned and raced back to town to report the inexplicable loss.

The disciples' attention was drawn back toward the madman as he began to regain consciousness. When he opened his eyes, the wild look was gone, replaced by a mixture of exhaustion and relief. Jesus motioned to a couple of the closest disciples and they apprehensively approached the man to help him to his feet. As they drew near, it became obvious that the first thing he needed was a rinse in the lake and a change of clothes.

As the morning sun climbed in the sky, the first spectators arrived from the nearby town to see what all the commotion was about. They had heard about the pigs, but when they got there they found an even bigger surprise. There was the town lunatic sitting among a group of strangers from across the lake - Jews by the look of them. Only, the crazy man didn't look so crazy all of a sudden. The erratic, violent behavior of this man was legendary throughout the Decapolis, the ten cities of this region. When the authorities had tried in the past to restrain him, he'd snapped the chains in his raw fury. Eventually, they'd given up trying to control him and had simply driven him out of town. Yet, here he was, dressed and sitting quietly among this group of Jews. As if that wasn't strange enough, there was an entire herd of pigs floating in the harbor. This couldn't be a coincidence.

When the men who had been tending the pigs showed up with the owner of the herd, they began to recount everything that had happened, explaining how Jesus' healing of this madman had coincided with the chaotic and ultimately fatal reaction of the pigs. A small group of them led by the owner finally approached Jesus and his disciples, all the while keeping a wary eye on the lunatic who was sitting with them. The owner asked one of the disciples what had happened and he simply replied, "My rabbi has freed this man from the evil spirits that held him captive."

The group of spectators couldn't help but be awed by the power of this Jewish rabbi, power that had enabled him to drive off the evil spirits that had tormented this man for so long. But they couldn't overlook the costly results – a whole herd of pigs wiped out in an instant. This rabbi was simply too disruptive and dangerous to remain in the region. It would be safer if he would just go back to where he'd come from. So they finally scraped together enough courage to approach Jesus and respectfully asked him to leave. To their surprise, Jesus consented and began to lead his disciples back toward the shore.

The group of spectators from the town watched from a distance as the disciples launched the boat and began to climb in. But as Jesus prepared to climb aboard, the man formerly known as Legion ran up to him. "Please, take me with you," he pleaded. There was nothing left for him here. All anybody would see him for was the lunatic that he'd been, but he wasn't that person anymore. Jesus had freed him from that nightmare and made a new man out of him. Yet, now that he was healed, he didn't want to face the mess that he'd created back home. It would be easier just to get in the boat and start over somewhere else.

Jesus understood the fear that lay behind this man's request, a fear of facing his past and the people he'd hurt. However, Jesus also understood the power of this man's testimony and the part he could play in advancing God's purpose and plans in this region. So, with compassion in his voice, Jesus shook his head and told the man, "Go home and tell your people what God has done for you. Tell them of the love and mercy he's poured out on you."

And with that, Jesus climbed up in the boat and the disciples began to row away, leaving the man formerly known as Legion standing on the shore.

★★★★★★

Every time I read this account in the Gospels, I can't help but be amazed that Jesus would sail all the way across the Sea of Galilee to interact with this one guy. Then, when the crowd pleads with him to leave, he would actually get back in the boat and sail away. It seems like such a waste of time, such an unproductive detour for the Son of God, whose public ministry only lasted a few years. And yet, it wasn't a waste of time, was it? For one thing, it radically altered the course of the demon-possessed man's life. He was salvaged from the graveyard and was given new purpose - to tell his people what God had done for him.

Yet, something we could easily overlook is the effect this man's testimony had in the Decapolis, these ten pagan cities on the far shore of the Sea of Galilee. Jesus sailed away upon the request of the frightened locals, but the next time he shows up in this region, he is thronged by crowds of people who bring their sick to him to be healed (Mark 7:31-8:10). He ends up ministering to them for three solid days and, at the end of his time there, he miraculously feeds some four-thousand people who have flocked to him from the surrounding countryside. It's a radically different reception than the first time he'd visited this part of the lake. And the only difference that we can point to for this change is the testimony of one man who had been freed from his bondage and given a renewed purpose in life.

The man formerly known as Legion had become an ambassador for Jesus to the very people who had previously ostracized him. What's more, the radical change that they saw in him no doubt gave credibility to his testimony. This one man became the key to unlocking the entire region to Jesus's ministry. Apparently Jesus's detour wasn't such a waste of time after all.

Embracing Our Purpose

If God could use a demon-possessed outcast to advance His kingdom purposes, imagine what He can do with us!

You and I have been created in God's image and we bear His indelible fingerprints. Admittedly, sin has marred both our ability to see that likeness as well as our ability to faithfully represent our Creator, but that's precisely why God sent Jesus to die for us – to undo the effects of sin in His representatives. Jesus' death paid the blood-debt that mankind's sins, from Adam onward, had accumulated, and in that supreme act of sacrifice, Jesus bought us out of slavery. Just as he'd done for the man who called himself Legion, Jesus released us from bondage and gave us a new lease on life.

In chapter seven, we looked at the way Jesus' death on the cross gave us the ability to find spiritual restoration. As Paul declared in his second letter to the Corinthians, "if anyone is in Christ, he is a new creation: the old has gone and the new has come" (2 Corinthians 5:17). By God's grace, we are no longer defined by our inability to live perfect lives; rather, we are remade by the blood of the perfect, spotless Son of God who gave his life for us. That said, simply being remade isn't the end of the story. There's more good news.

On the heels of proclaiming that in Christ we are new creations, Paul goes on to declare the restored purpose that we have in Him as well:

> All this is from God, who reconciled us to Himself through Christ and gave us the ministry of reconciliation: that God was reconciling the world to himself in Christ, not counting people's sins against them. And He has committed to us the message of reconciliation. We are, therefore, Christ's ambassadors, as though God were making His appeal through us" (2 Corinthians 5:18-20).

The amazing, sobering message of the gospel is that God has not merely remade us; He has also renewed the purpose for which He created us in the first place - to be His representatives.

When we give our hearts to Jesus and accept the gift of grace, we not only become adopted sons and daughters of God, we become living testaments to God's goodness and grace. We become our Father's representatives in our homes, our neighborhoods, our schools, our workplaces, and anywhere else that we go.

Out of the Stands and Onto the Field

Our Father's desire is that every single person who has been created in His image would hear the good news and have the opportunity to be reunited with Him. As Christ followers, we get to be the ones to share this good news with the world. We get to be ambassadors of the hope we've found in Jesus. It's quite an honor, but it's also a huge responsibility. I often feel inadequate for the task and I suspect that I'm not the only one that feels that way. For many believers, it's easier just to tithe to the church and financially support missionaries so that the "professional" Christians can do the work of representing God. But they're missing the point.

One of the commonly held misconceptions that people tend to carry around with them is that the only people God uses to advance His kingdom are the pastors in the churches and the missionaries overseas. It makes sense that people would think this way, given the way our churches are set up, with a select few leading the service while everyone else sits passively and watches. In a lot of ways, the church looks a lot like a sporting event, with the professional Christians (the paid staff and super-volunteers) on the field while the regular Christians sit in the stands and cheer them on. The problem with this picture is that God never intended for the majority of His children to live as passive observers. Rather, He calls each and every one of them to get out of the stands and onto the field. And He fills us with His Spirit to guide and empower us to do the ministry He's uniquely called us to do.

You might be thinking, "If we are all ministers and we are all called to be on the field rather than in the stands, then what is the purpose of the vocational church leaders?" Using the sports analogy, they become the coaches who train, equip and encourage the believers under their care to carry out the ministry that God has called each of them to do. Paul put it this way:

> Christ himself gave the apostles, the prophets, the
> evangelists, the pastors and teachers, to equip His

people for works of service, so that the body of
Christ may be built up until we all reach unity in the
faith and in the knowledge of the Son of God and
become mature, attaining to the whole measure of
the fullness of Christ. (Ephesians 4:11-13)

Vocational ministers have a part to play, but their part is not to be
the only ones on the field of ministry. In fact, to press this metaphor
just a little further, the coach's job is not to be on the field at all,
but rather on the sidelines, giving direction and encouragement to
those who are in the game. This means that the church services are
not the game itself, but the time-outs and scheduled breaks between
quarters when the players gather together to get on the same page.
They are the team meetings during those regular pauses in play,
when the coaches step in to remind the players of the bigger picture
and to help them recognize their part in the game.

The heart of Paul's message is that every single person that
has been adopted by God and filled with His Holy Spirit is an
ambassador of Christ in one way or another. While the vocational
ministers with their titles and pulpits and the missionaries living
overseas may be the most obvious representatives, the average
layperson is just as crucial to advancing the gospel into the world.
After all, a great number of people have little to no interest in
stepping foot into a church building, but God cares for them all
the same. And while He may call some of His kids to leave their
families, their friends and their homelands to go to a foreign
mission field, He calls the rest of us to the mission field just outside
our front door.

So how does God reach the regular patrons at the local coffee
shop? He dresses some of his kids up like baristas and has them
serve lattes with a side of love. How does He reach the single mom
who frequents the playground down the street? He dresses some
of His daughters up like moms and sends them to hang out at the
same playground. He dresses some of His kids up like attorneys

and has them tend to hurting souls in the legal field, and He dresses others like teachers and coaches and even students and then sends them to minister in the local schools.

Regardless of the roles you play or what you do to pay the bills, as a son or daughter of God, you are also a missionary into your own unique sphere of influence. You are an ambassador of hope and reconciliation, representing God to the people you come into contact with on a daily basis and reflecting the light of His love into a world filled with darkness and despair.

What's In Your Hand?

Of course, just because we are our Father's representatives doesn't necessarily mean we feel up to the task. How can admittedly imperfect people like us possibly hope to represent our holy God?

Moses asked a similar question when God appeared to him in a burning bush and called him to be His representative. When God told Moses that He wanted to use him to free His people from slavery in Egypt, Moses was incredulous and he said so. "Why me?" he asked. "Why would you choose a guy like me to talk with Pharaoh when someone, *anyone* would be a better choice?! I mean, I ran out of Egypt after I killed a guy. Why would you want a guy who's wanted for murder to represent you? How about my brother, Aaron? He's way more articulate than me."[55]

God told him not to worry, that He would be with him every step of the way. Still, Moses wasn't convinced that he was the right guy for the job, so he kept pushing: "What if they don't believe me or listen to me and say 'The LORD did not appear to you'?"(Exodus 4:1). Seems like a reasonable question.

God responded with a question of His own: "What's in your hand?"(4:2). Moses looked down and saw that he was holding his shepherd's staff. "Throw it down," God told him, and when Moses did, the staff turned into a snake. When he picked it back up it returned to a staff. This was one of the signs God gave Moses to prove that he truly had been sent by God and that his words were trustworthy.

Like Moses, I suspect that many of us feel completely inadequate to represent God. After all, we are intimately familiar with our flaws, which should naturally disqualify us from the job. On top of that, many of us don't feel mature enough in our faith to adequately share the gospel with others. And even if we could articulate the gospel with ease, why would anyone listen? The world seems more concerned with living the good life than worrying about the afterlife. So, with thoughts like these running through our mind, we resign ourselves to letting the professionals represent God. We're okay just sitting in the stands and cheering them on.

I suspect that God would ask us the same question that He asked Moses from the burning bush: "What do you have in your hand?"

Stop and consider that question for a moment. What has God given you that you could use to advance His kingdom?

For one, we each have our own testimony. It is one thing to tell someone that Jesus saves, but another thing altogether to show them how Jesus has saved you. In a day and age when everyone is selling something, when celebrities are paid to hawk stuff that they don't even use themselves, people are understandably skeptical. The world doesn't need another salesperson who doesn't use their own product. Thankfully, we're not trying to pawn something off on someone that we're not willing to buy ourselves. Our single greatest evidence that God is real and that He saves lives is our personal testimony. That's all the man formerly known as Legion had, and his testimony transformed an entire region and turned countless hearts toward Jesus.

What this world truly needs are real people who have real relationships with their Heavenly Father. I'm not talking pie-in-the-sky, "everything is just peachy" sort of relationships where we claim that everything is great and Jesus will make all of our troubles go away. As we saw in the last chapter, following Jesus doesn't guarantee us easy, care-free lives. Sometimes he leads us through some really dark valleys that bring a lot of pain with them and it's okay to admit that. In truth, the world is skeptical of anything that seems too perfect, too sanitized, so we might as well be honest. But we can't remain silent, because this world is passing away and people all around us that we know and love are dying right along with it. So how has God transformed your life? Why is the gospel good news for you?

Our testimony is perhaps the most powerful weapon in our arsenal, but it won't make much of an impact if nobody is listening. In a world full of competing perspectives, where people have grown naturally skeptical of anyone purporting to have access to the truth, we have to earn the right to be heard. After all, people don't really care what we know until they know that we care, right?! Jesus said that the world will know that we are his disciples by the way we love one another (John 13:35). Thankfully, our Father has given us the tools to put our love into action.

God has entrusted every single one of us with time, talents and treasures. While we often use these resources to make our lives more comfortable and enjoyable, they were never intended to be for us alone. We have been blessed in order to be a blessing and, if we are willing, God can use them to soften the hearts of those around us so that the gospel can take root in their lives. Admittedly, each of us has different quantities of time, talents and treasures; And while God doesn't hold us accountable for what He hasn't given us, He sure wants us to do something with what He has entrusted to our care.[56]

So what are you doing with the time He's given you? There are one-thousand-four-hundred-forty minutes every day. Are you investing them or are you frittering them away? And despite the fact that you are busy, are you interruptible? Reading over Jesus' life, he was tremendously busy, but he always seemed to be interruptible. When two blind men heard that Jesus was passing, they cried out for his merciful healing. The crowds tried to silence them, but Jesus stopped what he was doing, moved towards them, and then healed them (Matthew 20:29-34). Are you willing to pause from whatever you're doing when a kingdom-opportunity presents itself? Are you willing to slow down long enough to recognize the pain in the people all around you and then to actually stop and step into their pain with them?

What are you doing with the talents he's given you? Each of us has a unique blend of skills and abilities that God has entrusted to our care. Some are natural, others are learned, but all of them are valuable tools we can use to advance God's kingdom into our spheres of influence. For instance, my mother-in-law is a baby-whisperer. She has an uncanny ability to sooth even the most colicky child. So when Jessica, a single mother who lives down the street, was going through a particularly dark valley, my mother-in-law stepped in to watch her 5-month-old son. At first she just loved on the baby, praying over the little boy as he slept in her arms. Eventually, Jessica began to lower her defenses as well. My wife and I have lived near Jessica for four years, but she's always been pretty closed off to Jesus. However, over these last several months, she has been more open than ever. She has allowed my mother-in-law to speak into the pain of her broken marriage and even allowed her to pray over her on a couple occasions. God is using my mother-in-law's talent with children to powerfully shine the light of His love into Jessica's life. So what talents has God entrusted to your care? Would you be willing to use them to love on the people around you? Because God just might use them to unlock someone's heart to His love.

Finally, what treasures has God entrusted to your care? I'm not just talking about your bank account, though that's certainly one of our most obvious treasures. Anything we have is a potential tool that God could use to advance His kingdom. Growing up, my home was one of the most powerful evangelistic tools around, because my parents kept an open door and an extra space at the table. I can't even begin to count the number of friends from school that came face to face with the love of Jesus because my parents were so generous with their resources, not to mention their time and parental wisdom. So are you willing to allow God to use your home, your vehicles, your toys and your finances for His purposes? After all, it all belongs to Him anyway. We are merely stewards. As the rightful owner, He should have the right to determine how these things are used.

So I ask you, child of God, image-bearer of the King of Kings, are you willing to get out of the stands and onto the field? Are you willing to allow God to use what He has entrusted to your care to bring about His purposes in and through your life? As someone who's been ransomed from slavery and adopted into His great big spiritual family, are you willing to embrace your role as His representative, using whatever He's given you to do whatever He calls you to do?

That's the great adventure we call following Jesus. It's not always easy and it's not always comfortable, but from an eternal perspective, there's no better way to invest our lives.

> *Use Me, God. Show me how to take who I am,*
> *who I want to be, and what I can do,*
> *and use if for purpose greater than myself.*
> – Martin Luther King Jr.

Think About It –

- Do you have a hard time accepting that God wants to use you to advance His kingdom? Why or why not?

- Read 2 Corinthians 5:17-20. Why would God entrust the message of reconciliation to imperfect representatives like us?

- Who are the people God has uniquely placed in your sphere of influence that need to see the Gospel in your life?

- What's in your hand? What time, talents and treasures has God given you that could be used to advance His kingdom?

- Perhaps the most powerful tool we have for advancing the Gospel is our own testimony. How has God transformed your life? Why is the Gospel good news for you?

ENDNOTES

1   All Biblical citations are from the New International Version unless otherwise indicated.

2   Isaiah 43:7 states that "we have been made for His glory," and many would argue that God created solely to glorify Himself. While all of creation is, indeed, full of His glory (Isaiah 6:3), this glory is not a product of creation. God was and is glorious without us and, as Jesus pointed out, He possessed His glory "before the world was made" (John 17:5). Therefore, creation does not produce glory for God, it simply reflects His glory, reveals it through the grand dance of galaxies and the minute complexity of the cells in our bodies.

3   The term helper (Hebrew: *ezer*) does not connote a secondary position. In fact, sixteen times in the Old Testament, God Himself is referred to as our *ezer*. So rather than suggesting an inferior position, this term is used to point out that women have been designed by God to be a strong and capable counterpart to men, his partner in dominion over creation.

4   Isaiah 46:10

5   CS Lewis, *Mere Christianity*, pg. 48.

6   God never stated that death would come through merely touching the fruit of the tree.

7   While the Genesis account simply refers to this creature as a serpent, other biblical passages reveal that the serpent was Satan. Thus, the curse that God imposes foreshadows the struggle between mankind and Satan. This struggle would ultimately culminate in the showdown between Jesus and Satan – Satan would bite at his heel, but Jesus would ultimately crush his head. Jesus would triumph over Satan by conquering death and redeeming mankind from the clutches of sin, and Revelation 20 states that Christ will one day defeat him once and for all.

8   God tells her, *"Your desire will be for your husband, and he will rule over you"* (Genesis 3:16). When we read that her "desire" will be for her husband,

we might interpret this to mean that Eve will simply be attracted to him and want to spend time with him. However, that's not what the original word meant. The term desire here isn't one of attraction or romance. Rather, it speaks to the woman's desire to control her husband, to gain mastery over him any way that she can. The same word is used in Genesis 4, when God warns Cain that *"sin is crouching at your door – it desires to have you, but you must master it"* (Genesis 4:7). In other words, the woman's desire will be to control, manipulate, and ultimately fix her husband, rather than trusting and following his lead. Similarly, God curses the way the husband relates to his wife. The term "rule" is the same one used of kings over their subjects. In other words, the husband will seek to dominate his wife and get his way through sheer force of will. So one of the effects of the Fall is a fracturing of marital relationships. Instead of a harmonious, mutually encouraging marriage, suddenly the relationship is filled with strife, discord and power struggles. The wife will strive to control and fix her defective husband while he tries to dominate the marital relationship and dictate how his wife lives.

9   I am indebted to Mike Erre, my friend and mentor, for his insights on the redemptive aspects of the curses.

10 Thomas Stanley and William Danko, *The Millionaire Next Door, The Surprising Secrets of America's Wealth*, MJF Books, New York 1996 – p.8

11 https://www.valuepenguin.com/average-credit-card-debt/ (7/2/2017)

12 https://www.gobankingrates.com/personal-finance/data-americans-savings/ (9/19/2016)

13 David Ramsey, *The Total Money Makeover: A Proven Plan for Financial Fitness*

14 Paul Laurence Dunbar, *Lyrics of Lowly Life*, Dodd, Mead, and Company,1896.

15 Leslie Vernick, *The Emotionally Destructive Relationship: Seeing It, Stopping It, Surviving It*

16 https://www.shirleymaclaine.com/articles/aging/article-265

17 Robert Frost, *Mountain Interval*. New York: Henry Holt and Company, 1920.

18 Nathaniel Hawthorne. *The Scarlet Letter*, Bantam Books, 1986.

19 http://www.pbs.org/wgbh/roadshow/archive/199705A06.html

20 http://www.pbs.org/wgbh/roadshow/archive/199708A13.html

21 http://www.pbs.org/wgbh/roadshow/video/BF_199708A13.html

22 We will explore this point in greater detail in chapter 10.

23 Leviticus 11:44; 1 Peter 1:16

24 The Hebrew Scriptures, which Christians refer to as the Old Testament.

25 For instance, Rabbinic teaching declared that if they could get all of Israel to keep just one Sabbath perfectly, then the Messiah would come immediately (Shemot Rabba 25:121; Yerushalmi, Ta'anit 1:10). So they legislated everything: from how far someone could walk on the Sabbath (about 2,000 paces) to what constituted work. In the end, Rabbis came up with thirty-nine major categories (with hundreds of subcategories) of what constituted work and should, therefore, be forbidden on the Sabbath. They focused on the letter of the Law, but forgot about the heart of it. It's no wonder that Jesus came into conflict with their rules as often as he did.

26 John Newton, *Amazing Grace*, 1779.

27 Amazingly, this prophetic declaration was written around 700 years before Jesus died on the cross for our sins!

28 There is nothing magical about these words, nor is there a set prayer you need to pray. In fact, every time I lead someone in the sinner's prayer, it differs slightly, though the heart of the prayer is still the same. So feel free to use your own words to accept his gift of grace and to take that first step of following him.

29 Thomas B. Costain, *The Three Edwards*, Popular Library, 1968. Page 191.

30 Helen H. Lemmel, *Turn Your Eyes Upon Jesus*, 1922.

31 In Greek the word is Paraclete, meaning "one who comes alongside."

32 See Ezekiel 8-10. Yet, even in the midst of Israel's disobedience, which ultimately led to their expulsion from the Promised Land at the hands of foreign enemies, God promises in Ezekiel 11 that He would not leave them in captivity forever, but would one day gather the remnant from where they have been scattered. And He promises that on that day, "I will give them an undivided heart and put a new spirit in them; I will remove from them their heart of stone and give them a heart of flesh. Then they will follow my decrees and be careful to keep my laws. They will be my people, and I will be their God" (*Ezekiel 11:19–20*).

33 Matthew 27:51

34 http://www.desiringgod.org/articles/the-gospel-shadow-of-adoption-amos-s-story,

35 See Romans 5:12-14

36 1 John 3:1

37 See 2 Corinthians 1:22 and Ephesians 1:13-14

38 Douglas Moo, *The NIV Application Commentary: Romans*, Zondervan, Grand Rapids, MI, 2000; p. 261.

39   In fact, all three New Testament books that discuss our adoption as sons and daughters of God were written to a predominantly gentile audience: Romans, Galatians and Ephesians.

40   William Barclay, *The Letter to the Romans*, Westminster Press, Philadelphia, PA, 1975; p. 106.

41   William Barclay, *The Letters to the Galatians and Ephesians*, Westminster John Knox Press, 2002. P 203

42   Roman Historian William Ramsay explains that "a formerly prevalent Greek law had persisted under the Roman Empire... It actually lays down the principle that a man can never put away an adopted son, and that he cannot put away a real son without good ground. It is remarkable that the adopted son should have a stronger position than the son by birth, yet it was so." W.M. Ramsay, *A Historical Commentary on St. Paul's Epistle to the Galatians*, Baker Book House, Grand Rapids, MI, reprinted 1979; p. 353.

43   Again, I am indebted to Mike Erre for his insights on this subject.

44   Lee Strobel, *The Case for the Real Jesus: A Journalist Investigates Current Attacks on the Identity of Christ*.

45   See Romans 6:15-18

46   For more information on what the Church in Costa Mesa has and is doing to address our city's needs, go to www.wearetrellis.com. One book that was particularly helpful in our transformation from competing churches to a unified body of believers is *To Transform a City: Whole Church, Whole Gospel, Whole City*, by Eric Swanson and Sam Williams.

47   Ken Auletta, "The Lost Tycoon," *New Yorker Magazine*, April 23, 2001.

48   Quoted in *What Are You Living For?" Investing Your Life in What Matters Most*, by Pat Williams and Jim Denney.

49   Ibid.

50   Ibid.

51   See Exodus 20:5 and 34:6-7.

52   See 2 Corinthians 11:23-33 for a fuller list of the things Paul endured in the name of advancing the gospel to the Gentiles.

53   After the Fall, God tweaked creation, intentionally hindering it from being the idyllic world that He'd created it to be so that mankind would be pointed back toward Him (Genesis 3:17-19). In his letter to the Romans, Paul acknowledged this intentional frustration of nature and looked forward to the day when God would make all things new (Romans 8:20-21).

54 This statement is probably a mistaken paraphrase of 1 Corinthians 10:13 – "God is faithful; he will not let you be tempted beyond what you can bear. But when you are tempted, he will also provide a way out so that you can endure it." But Paul's focus in this passage is on our temptations, not our trials.

55 My very loose paraphrase of Moses' initial reaction, as recorded in Exodus 3:11 and 4:10-13

56 I think of the parable of the talents, where each servant was given a different amount of money. The master never punished the man who had two talents for earning less than the man who had five, but he came down hard on the man who buried his single talent in the ground and did nothing with it (Matthew 25:14-30).

ACKNOWLEDGEMENTS

No book is written in a vacuum and this one is certainly no exception. There is virtually nothing contained in these pages for which I can claim full credit. My insights have been collected through countless sermons, books and conversations. They have been honed through the patient investment of friends and mentors who have walked alongside me on this adventure called "following Jesus."

Specifically, I'd like to thank my wife and sons, who have taught me more about unconditional love than any book or sermon ever could. I'd like to thank my parents, who introduced me to Jesus and patiently loved me no matter how impulsive I acted. Then there's all the other men and women who invested in me throughout my life. There are more names than I have space to write, but you know who you are and I am grateful for the indelible fingerprints you've left on my life. Mike Erre, thank you for the countless insights I've gleaned from you. I've given you credit for a few, but no doubt there are many more that I borrowed from you and unwittingly claimed as my own. And Brennan Manning, my hope is that this book will impact a generation in the same way that *Abba's Child* impacted me.

Thank you to those who have walked with me through this writing process: some of you read the initial chapters in their rough and undeveloped state and helped me to hone it into something readable. Others have helped encourage me along the way: Michelle Anthony, I'm looking at you. Your words of encouragement were a fresh breeze when I found myself wandering in the publishing wilderness. Brenda, thank you for believing in this project and bringing your marketing talents to bear on it. And Dee, thank you for regularly asking me, "Did you write something today?" You truly spurred me on.

Luke, thank you for designing my favorite book cover ever. This is one book that I'd like people to judge by its cover. Arpit, thank you for taking new headshots. And thank you to all the people at Westbow Press who brought this project through to completion.

Finally, thank you Father God for loving me and allowing me to be your royal representative. I am grateful that you use imperfect people to pour out your perfect love. I pray that you use these chapters to raise up another generation of fully-committed followers who know who they are and what you've made them to do. To you be all glory.

Made in the USA
San Bernardino, CA
31 May 2018